# Get Ready!

## FOR STANDARDIZED TESTS

## READING, GRADE THREE

**Other Books in the *Get Ready!* Series:**

TEST PREPARATION SERIES

# Get Ready!

## FOR STANDARDIZED TESTS

## READING, GRADE THREE

Joanne Baker

Carol Turkington
Series Editor

**McGraw-Hill**

New York   Chicago   San Francisco
Lisbon   London   Madrid   Mexico City
Milan   New Delhi   San Juan   Seoul
Singapore   Sydney   Toronto

**Library of Congress Cataloging-in-Publication Data**

Get ready! for standardized tests. Reading.
    p. cm.—(Test preparation series)
  Contents:—[v. 2] Grade two / Louise Ulrich—[v. 3] Grade three / Joanne Baker—
[v. 4] Grade four / Kris Callahan.
  ISBN 0-07-137406-X (pbk. : v. 2)—ISBN 0-07-137407-8 (pbk. : v. 3)—ISBN
0-07-137408-6 (pbk. : v. 4)
  1. Achievement tests—United States—Study guides.  2. Reading (Elementary)—United
States—Evaluation.  3. Reading (Elementary)—Parent participation—United States.  I.
Ulrich, Louise.  II. Test preparation series (McGraw-Hill Companies)

  LB3060.22 .G48   2001
  372.126'2—dc21

2001030896

*McGraw-Hill*

*A Division of The **McGraw·Hill** Companies*

1 2 3 4 5 6 7 8 9 0 COU/COU 0 9 8 7 6 5 4 3 2 1

ISBN 0-07-137407-8

*This book was set in New Century Schoolbook by Inkwell Publishing Services.*

*Printed and bound by Courier.*

McGraw-Hill books are available at special quantity discounts to use as premiums
and sales promotions, or for use in corporate training programs. For more information, please write to the Director of Special Sales, McGraw-Hill, Professional
Publishing, Two Penn Plaza, New York, NY 10121-2298. Or contact your local bookstore.

To my husband, Bill; sons, Josh and Peter; Mother; and most especially to Grandma Ziegler, who first introduced me to the joys of reading.

*Joanne Baker*

# Contents

# SKILLS CHECKLIST

| MY CHILD ... | HAS LEARNED | IS WORKING ON |
|---|---|---|
| VOCABULARY | | |
| ANALOGIES | | |
| ANTONYMS | | |
| SYNONYMS | | |
| HOMOPHONES | | |
| WORD MEANINGS IN CONTEXT | | |
| CONSONANTS | | |
| VOWELS | | |
| BLENDS | | |
| BASE WORDS | | |
| ROOT WORDS | | |
| SUFFIXES | | |
| PREFIXES | | |
| COMPOUND WORDS | | |
| CAPITALIZATION | | |
| PUNCTUATION | | |
| PARTS OF SPEECH | | |
| MAIN IDEA AND DETAILS | | |
| SEQUENCE | | |
| CHARACTERS AND SETTINGS | | |
| PREDICTING OUTCOMES | | |
| DRAWING CONCLUSIONS | | |
| CAUSE AND EFFECT | | |
| FACTS AND OPINION | | |
| REALITY VERSUS FANTASY | | |
| BIOGRAPHY | | |
| POETRY | | |
| ALPHABETICAL ORDER TO THE THIRD LETTER | | |
| DICTIONARY SKILLS | | |
| GRAPHS | | |
| RECOGNIZING PARTS OF A BOOK | | |

# Introduction

Almost all of us have taken standardized tests in school. We spent several days bubbling-in answers, shifting in our seats. No one ever told us why we took the tests or what they would do with the results. We just took them and never heard about them again.

Today many parents aren't aware they are entitled to see their children's permanent records and, at a reasonable cost, to obtain copies of any information not protected by copyright, including testing scores. Late in the school year, most parents receive standardized test results with confusing bar charts and detailed explanations of scores that few people seem to understand.

In response to a series of negative reports on the state of education in this country, Americans have begun to demand that something be done to improve our schools. We have come to expect higher levels of accountability as schools face the competing pressures of rising educational expectations and declining school budgets. High-stakes standardized tests are rapidly becoming the main tool of accountability for students, teachers, and school administrators. If students' test scores don't continually rise, teachers and principals face the potential loss of school funding and, ultimately, their jobs. Summer school and private after-school tutorial program enrollments are swelling with students who have not met score standards or who, everyone agrees, could score higher.

While there is a great deal of controversy about whether it is appropriate for schools to use standardized tests to make major decisions about individual students, it appears likely that standardized tests are here to stay. They will be used to evaluate students, teachers, and the schools; schools are sure to continue to use students' test scores to demonstrate their accountability to the community.

The purposes of this guide are to acquaint you with the types of standardized tests your children may take; to help you understand the test results; and to help you work with your children in skill areas that are measured by standardized tests so they can perform as well as possible.

## Types of Standardized Tests

The two major types of group standardized tests are *criterion-referenced tests* and *norm-referenced tests*. Think back to when you learned to tie your shoes. First Mom or Dad showed you how to loosen the laces on your shoe so that you could insert your foot; then they showed you how to tighten the laces—but not too tight. They showed you how to make bows and how to tie a knot. All the steps we just described constitute what is called a *skills hierarchy:* a list of skills from easiest to most difficult that are related to some goal, such as tying a shoelace.

Criterion-referenced tests are designed to determine at what level students are performing on various skills hierarchies. These tests assume that development of skills follows a sequence of steps. For example, if you were teaching shoelace tying, the skills hierarchy might appear this way:

1. Loosen laces.
2. Insert foot.
3. Tighten laces.
4. Make loops with both lace ends.
5. Tie a square knot.

Criterion-referenced tests try to identify how far along the skills hierarchy the student has progressed. There is no comparison against anyone else's score, only against an expected skill level. The main question criterion-referenced tests ask is: "Where is this child in the development of this group of skills?"

Norm-referenced tests, in contrast, are typically constructed to compare children in their abilities as to different skills areas. Although the experts who design test items may be aware of skills hierarchies, they are more concerned with how much of some skill the child has mastered, rather than at what level on the skills hierarchy the child is.

Ideally, the questions on these tests range from very easy items to those that are impossibly difficult. The essential feature of norm-referenced tests is that scores on these measures can be compared to scores of children in similar groups. They answer this question: "How does the child compare with other children of the same age or grade placement in the development of this skill?"

This book provides strategies for increasing your child's scores on both standardized norm-referenced and criterion-referenced tests.

## The Major Standardized Tests

Many criterion-referenced tests currently in use are created locally or (at best) on a state level,

and there are far too many of them to go into detail here about specific tests. However, children prepare for them in basically the same way they do for norm-referenced tests.

A very small pool of norm-referenced tests is used throughout the country, consisting primarily of the Big Five:

- California Achievement Tests (CTB/McGraw-Hill)
- Iowa Tests of Basic Skills (Riverside)
- Metropolitan Achievement Test (Harcourt-Brace & Company)
- Stanford Achievement Test (Psychological Corporation)
- TerraNova [formerly Comprehensive Test of Basic Skills] (McGraw-Hill)

These tests use various terms for the academic skills areas they assess, but they generally test several types of reading, language, and mathematics skills, along with social studies and science. They may include additional assessments, such as of study and reference skills.

## How States Use Standardized Tests

Despite widespread belief and practice to the contrary, group standardized tests are designed to assess and compare the achievement of groups. They are *not* designed to provide detailed diagnostic assessments of individual students. (For detailed individual assessments, children should be given individual diagnostic tests by properly qualified professionals, including trained guidance counselors, speech and language therapists, and school psychologists.) Here are examples of the types of questions group standardized tests are designed to answer:

- How did the reading achievement of students at Valley Elementary School this year compare with their reading achievement last year?

- How did math scores at Wonderland Middle School compare with those of students at Parkside Middle School this year?

- As a group, how did Hilltop High School students compare with the national averages in the achievement areas tested?

- How did the district's first graders' math scores compare with the district's fifth graders' math scores?

The fact that these tests are designed primarily to test and compare groups doesn't mean that test data on individual students isn't useful. It does mean that when we use these tests to diagnose individual students, we are using them for a purpose for which they were not designed.

Think of group standardized tests as being similar to health fairs at the local mall. Rather than check into your local hospital and spend thousands of dollars on full, individual tests for a wide range of conditions, you can go from station to station and take part in different health screenings. Of course, one would never diagnose heart disease or cancer on the basis of the screening done at the mall. At most, suspicious results on the screening would suggest that you need to visit a doctor for a more complete examination.

In the same way, group standardized tests provide a way of screening the achievement of many students quickly. Although you shouldn't diagnose learning problems solely based on the results of these tests, the results can tell you that you should think about referring a child for a more definitive, individual assessment.

An individual student's group test data should be considered only a point of information. Teachers and school administrators may use standardized test results to support or question hypotheses they have made about students; but these scores must be used alongside other information, such as teacher comments, daily work, homework, class test grades, parent observations, medical needs, and social history.

## Valid Uses of Standardized Test Scores

Here are examples of appropriate uses of test scores for individual students:

- Mr. Cone thinks that Samantha, a third grader, is struggling in math. He reviews her file and finds that her first- and second-grade standardized test math scores were very low. Her first- and second-grade teachers recall episodes in which Samantha cried because she couldn't understand certain math concepts, and mention that she was teased by other children, who called her "Dummy." Mr. Cone decides to refer Samantha to the school assistance team to determine whether she should be referred for individual testing for a learning disability related to math.

- The local college wants to set up a tutoring program for elementary school children who are struggling academically. In deciding which youngsters to nominate for the program, the teachers consider the students' averages in different subjects, the degree to which students seem to be struggling, parents' reports, and standardized test scores.

- For the second year in a row, Gene has performed poorly on the latest round of standardized tests. His teachers all agree that Gene seems to have some serious learning problems. They had hoped that Gene was immature for his class and that he would do better this year; but his dismal grades continue. Gene is referred to the school assistance team to determine whether he should be sent to the school psychologist for assessment of a possible learning handicap.

## Inappropriate Use of Standardized Test Scores

Here are examples of how schools have sometimes used standardized test results inappropriately:

- Mr. Johnson groups his students into reading groups solely on the basis of their standardized test scores.

- Ms. Henry recommends that Susie be held back a year because she performed poorly on the standardized tests, despite strong grades on daily assignments, homework, and class tests.

- Gerald's teacher refers him for consideration in the district's gifted program, which accepts students using a combination of intelligence test scores, achievement test scores, and teacher recommendations. Gerald's intelligence test scores were very high. Unfortunately, he had a bad cold during the week of the standardized group achievement tests and was taking powerful antihistamines, which made him feel sleepy. As a result, he scored too low on the achievement tests to qualify.

The public has come to demand increasingly high levels of accountability for public schools. We demand that schools test so that we have hard data with which to hold the schools accountable. But too often, politicians and the public place more faith in the test results than is justified. Regardless of whether it's appropriate to do so and regardless of the reasons schools use standardized test results as they do, many schools base crucial programming and eligibility decisions on scores from group standardized tests. It's to your child's advantage, then, to perform as well as possible on these tests.

## Two Basic Assumptions

The strategies we present in this book come from two basic assumptions:

1. Most students can raise their standardized test scores.

2. Parents can help their children become stronger in the skills the tests assess.

This book provides the information you need to learn what skill areas the tests measure, what general skills your child is being taught in a particular grade, how to prepare your child to take the tests, and what to do with the results. In the appendices you will find information to help you decipher test interpretations; a listing of which states currently require what tests; and additional resources to help you help your child to do better in school and to prepare for the tests.

## A Word about Coaching

This guide is *not* about coaching your child. When we use the term *coaching* in referring to standardized testing, we mean trying to give someone an unfair advantage, either by revealing beforehand what exact items will be on the test or by teaching "tricks" that will supposedly allow a student to take advantage of some detail in how the tests are constructed.

Some people try to coach students in shrewd test-taking strategies that take advantage of how the tests are supposedly constructed rather than strengthening the students' skills in the areas tested. Over the years, for example, many rumors have been floated about "secret formulas" that test companies use.

This type of coaching emphasizes ways to help students obtain scores they didn't earn—to get something for nothing. Stories have appeared in the press about teachers who have coached their students on specific questions, parents who have tried to obtain advance copies of tests, and students who have written down test questions after taking standardized tests and sold them to others. Because of the importance of test security, test companies and states aggressively prosecute those who attempt to violate test security—and they should do so.

## How to Raise Test Scores

Factors that are unrelated to how strong students are but that might artificially lower test scores include anything that prevents students from making scores that accurately describe their actual abilities. Some of those factors are:

- giving the tests in uncomfortably cold or hot rooms;
- allowing outside noises to interfere with test taking; and
- reproducing test booklets in such small print or with such faint ink that students can't read the questions.

Such problems require administrative attention from both the test publishers, who must make sure that they obtain their norms for the tests under the same conditions students face when they take the tests; and school administrators, who must ensure that conditions under which their students take the tests are as close as possible to those specified by the test publishers.

Individual students also face problems that can artificially lower their test scores, and parents can do something about many of these problems. Stomach aches, headaches, sleep deprivation, colds and flu, and emotional upsets due to a recent tragedy are problems that might call for the student to take the tests during make-up sessions. Some students have physical conditions such as muscle-control problems, palsies, or difficulty paying attention that require work over many months or even years before students can obtain accurate test scores on standardized tests. And, of course, some students just don't take the testing seriously or may even intentionally perform poorly. Parents can help their children overcome many of these obstacles to obtaining accurate scores.

Finally, with this book parents are able to help their children raise their scores by:

- increasing their familiarity (and their comfort level) with the types of questions on standardized tests;
- drills and practice exercises to increase their skill in handling the kinds of questions they will meet; and

- providing lots of fun ways for parents to help their children work on the skill areas that will be tested.

## Test Questions

The favorite type of question for standardized tests is the multiple-choice question. For example:

1. The first President of the United States was:

   A Abraham Lincoln

   B Martin Luther King, Jr.

   C George Washington

   D Thomas Jefferson

The main advantage of multiple-choice questions is that it is easy to score them quickly and accurately. They lend themselves to optical scanning test forms, on which students fill in bubbles or squares and the forms are scored by machine. Increasingly, companies are moving from paper-based testing to computer-based testing, using multiple-choice questions.

The main disadvantage of multiple-choice questions is that they restrict test items to those that can be put in that form. Many educators and civil rights advocates have noted that the multiple-choice format only reveals a superficial understanding of the subject. It's not possible with multiple-choice questions to test a student's ability to construct a detailed, logical argument on some issue or to explain a detailed process. Although some of the major tests are beginning to incorporate more subjectively scored items, such as short answer or essay questions, the vast majority of test items continue to be in multiple-choice format.

In the past, some people believed there were special formulas or tricks to help test-takers determine which multiple-choice answer was the correct one. There may have been some truth to *some* claims for past tests. Computer analyses of some past tests revealed certain biases in how tests were constructed. For example, the old advice to pick *D* when in doubt appears to have been valid for some past tests. However, test publishers have become so sophisticated in their ability to detect patterns of bias in the formulation of test questions and answers that they now guard against it aggressively.

In Chapter 1, we provide information about general test-taking considerations, with advice on how parents can help students overcome testing obstacles. The rest of the book provides information to help parents help their children strengthen skills in the tested areas.

Joseph Harris, Ph.D.

# Test-Taking Basics

It's almost certain that some time during the 12 years your child spends in school, he will face a standardized testing situation. Some schools test every year, some test every other year, but at some point your child will be assessed by taking a standardized test. How well your child does on such a test can be related to many things—did he get plenty of rest the night before? Is he anxious in testing situations? Did he get confused when filling in the answer sheets and make a mechanical mistake?

These factors unrelated to the test content are the reason educators emphasize that a child's score on a standardized test shouldn't be used as the sole judge of how that child is learning and developing. Instead, the scores should be evaluated as only one part of the educational picture, the other parts being the child's classroom performance and overall areas of strength and weakness. Your child won't pass or fail a standardized test, but a test can often reveal a general pattern of strengths and weaknesses.

## What This Book Can Do

This book is not designed to help your child artificially inflate his scores on a standardized test. Instead, its purpose is to help you understand what typical skills are taught in a third-grade class and what a typical third grader can be expected to know by the end of the third year. It also presents lots of fun activities that you can

use at home to work with your child in particular skill areas that may be a bit weak.

This book is not designed to replace your child's teacher but rather to help you work together with the school as a team to help your child succeed.

In helping your child prepare for school, keep in mind that endless drilling is not the best way to help him improve. While most children want to do well and please their teachers and parents, they already spend about seven hours a day in school. Extracurricular activities, homework, music, and sports practice take up more time. Try to use the activities in this book to stimulate and support your child's work at school without overwhelming him.

Children entering the third grade are more able to think independently and are thus able to confront more complex material in school than they were able to earlier. As a result of the changes in the way he thinks, you will find that your child's class spends less time dealing with concrete learning. You'll find your child is better able to understand the multiple meanings of words, to remember complex material, and to begin to summarize effectively. You should use the information presented in this book in conjunction with schoolwork to help develop your child's essential skills in reading, grammar, and writing. All of these skills will be reflected in the third-grade curriculum. Remember, however, that not all children learn things at the same rate. What may be typical for one third grader is certainly not for another.

## How to Use This Book

There are many different ways to use this book. Some children are quite strong in some verbal areas but need a bit of help in others. Perhaps your child is a whiz at vocabulary but has more trouble with reading comprehension. Focus your attention and spend more time on those skills that need some work.

You'll see in each chapter an introductory explanation of the material in the chapter. That is followed by a summary of what a typical child in third grade should be expected to know and how advanced she should be in a particular skill by the end of the year. Next, you'll find an explanation of how standardized tests may assess that skill and what your child might expect to see on a typical test.

This introduction is followed in each chapter by an extensive section featuring interesting, fun, or unusual activities you can do with your child to reinforce the skills presented in the chapter. Most use only inexpensive items found around the home, and many are suitable for car trips, waiting rooms, and restaurants.

We've included sample questions at the end of each section that are designed to help familiarize your child with the types of questions found on a typical standardized test. These questions do **not** measure your child's proficiency in any given content area—but if you notice your child is having trouble with a particular question, you can use that information to figure out what skills you need to focus on.

## Basic Test-Taking Strategies

Sometimes children score lower than they should on standardized tests because they approach testing in an inefficient way. There are things you can do before the test—and that your child can do during the test—to make sure he does as well as he can.

### Before the Test

Perhaps the most effective step you can take to prepare your child for standardized tests is to be patient. Remember that no matter how much pressure you put on your child, she won't learn certain skills until she is physically, mentally, and emotionally ready to do so. You've got to walk a delicate line between challenging and pressuring your child. If you see your child isn't making progress or is getting frustrated, it may be time to lighten up.

**Don't Change the Routine.** Many experts offer mistaken advice about how to prepare children for a test, such as recommending that children go to bed early the night before or eat a high-protein breakfast on the morning of the test.

It's a better idea not to alter your child's routine at all right before the test. If your child isn't used to going to bed early, then sending him off at 7:30 p.m. the night before a test will only make it harder for him to get to sleep by the normal time. If he is used to eating an orange or a piece of toast for breakfast, forcing him to down a platter of fried eggs and bacon will only make him feel sleepy or uncomfortable.

**Neatness.** Children sometimes make mistakes in the way they fill in an answer sheet on a standardized test, and these mistakes can really make a difference in the final test results. It pays to give your child some practice filling in answer sheets. Watch how neatly your child can fill in the bubbles, squares, and rectangles on the next page. If he overlaps the lines, makes a lot of erase marks, or presses the pencil too hard, try having him practice with pages of bubbles. You can easily create sheets of capital *O*'s, squares, and rectangles that your child can practice filling in. If he gets bored doing that, have him color in detailed pictures in coloring books or complete connect-the-dots pages.

### During the Test

There are some approaches to standardized testing that have been shown to make some

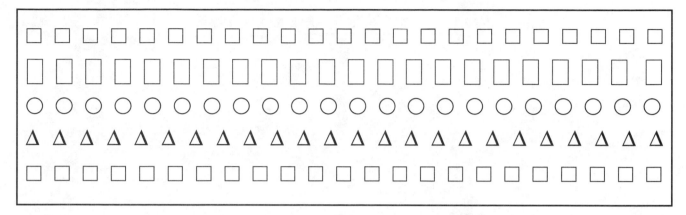

degree of improvement in a score. Discuss the following strategies with your child from time to time.

**Bring Extra Pencils.** You don't want your child spending valuable testing time jumping up to sharpen a pencil. Send along plenty of extra, well-sharpened pencils so that he won't need to find or sharpen pencils during the test.

**Listen Carefully.** You wouldn't believe how many errors kids make because they did not listen to instructions or pay attention to demonstrations. Some children mark the wrong form, fill in the bubbles incorrectly, or skip to the wrong section. Others simply forget to put their names on the answer sheets. Many mark their answer sheet before checking to see that they are marking the right bubble.

**Read the Entire Question First.** Some children get so excited about the test that they begin filling in bubbles before they finish reading the entire question. The last few words in a question sometimes give the most important clues to the correct answer.

**Read Carefully.** In their desire to finish first, many children tend to select the first answer that seems right to them without thoroughly reading all the responses and choosing the very

best answer. Make sure your child understands the importance of evaluating all the answers before choosing one.

**Skip Difficult Items; Return to Them Later.** Many children will sit and worry about a hard question, spending so much time on one problem that they never get to problems that they would be able to answer correctly if they only had enough time. Explain to your child that he can always return to a knotty question once he finishes the section.

**Refer to Pictures for Clues.** Tell your child not to overlook the pictures in the test booklets, which may reveal valuable clues that can help him find the correct answers. Students can also find clues to correct answers by looking at descriptions, wording, and other information in the questions themselves.

**Use Key Words.** Have your child try to identify the key words in the test questions.

**Eliminate Answer Choices.** Just as in the wildly successful TV show *Who Wants to Be a Millionaire,* remind your child that it's a good idea to narrow down his choices among multiple-choice options by eliminating answers he knows can't possibly be true.

## CHAPTER 2

# Vocabulary

The ability to recognize the meaning of words, and to be able to analyze them effectively, is an important part of being a good reader. As children become more sophisticated readers, they begin to recognize that words are built with predictable spelling patterns. The early years in school are a time of tremendous brain development, particularly in the areas that control how we speak to others and how we interpret what they say to us. This is the reason that you have seen such tremendous growth in vocabulary in first and second grade, which will continue in third.

## Vocabulary

### What Third Graders Should Know

The development of your child's vocabulary plays an important role in her ability to progress in reading. By now, your child is learning to recognize synonyms, antonyms, and homophones and to understand what each word means and how it relates to a sentence. Your child also should be able to identify the meaning of words in context and to understand the basics of analogies.

### What You and Your Child Can Do

There is a great deal you can do at home to boost your child's acquisition of words, both through the language you use and in fun games you play together. But try not to make vocabulary development drudgery—it doesn't have to be! Try to create an atmosphere that fosters exploration. Don't just hand your third grader a worksheet—instead, invite her to join you in the enjoyment of words.

**Read and Read Some More!** Your third grader is not too old to read to. If you want your child to have an effective vocabulary, the best way to do that is to continue to read to her. Read every day, and let her read aloud to you as well. Choose books on a wide range of subjects, and let your child choose her own. Be alert for her special hobbies or interests, and then provide books on that topic. You don't have to buy books; you can borrow as many as your child can read from the local library.

**Play Commercial Games.** There are many commercial games that are good for boosting vocabulary. Games such as *Concentration* or *Password* are old favorites and can help boost vocabulary. *Scrabble* (or *Scrabble Junior*) is another great choice.

**Take a Trip.** You don't have to journey to Paris to find interesting places to take your third grader. On regular outings—to a museum, planetarium, or zoo—encourage her to read the materials available. Help her expand her interests because a curious child with lots of stimulation will almost automatically have a larger vocabulary. If your child is interested in the ocean, take her to a nearby aquarium. If she's interested in trains, take her to the local station. If she likes animals, join the local zoo society or arrange to observe a veterinarian at work. Perhaps she could help out at a local kennel or stable. While it may not seem that these trips involve reading, what you're doing is expanding her experience and triggering her interest, all of which will eventually improve her vocabulary.

**Talk to Your Child.** Reading isn't the only way to boost vocabulary, conversation will also do the trick. In fact, the more varied and complex the language she hears, the better her vocabulary will be. It's a fact: Children with a strong vocabulary tend to have parents with a strong vocabulary. Don't despair if your own vocabulary isn't the best. If her environment is stimulating, your child's vocabulary will improve.

**Play Stump the Family.** Each day, assign a member of your family to look up the meaning of one new word, and then use the word to try to stump the family at dinner. On her day, help your third grader look through a dictionary to find an unusual word. See if anyone can guess what the word means.

**Build a Scaffold.** One way parents can boost a child's word usage is to use a verbal *scaffold*— that is, use a complex word and then define it in simpler terms right after. For example, Sara's mother says: "Oh, the honey is *crystallizing*. It's forming little hard bits that won't melt." Children with the best vocabularies tend to have parents who automatically "scaffold" their sentences. E. B. White (*Charlotte's Web*) is one writer known for scaffolding well.

**Define It.** Of course, it's also fine if you simply define words outright: "Your grandfather was *ambidextrous*. That means he could use his right hand just as well as he could use his left." Don't automatically use the simplest words to talk to your child. Speak to her as if she were older; you might be surprised at how fast her vocabulary improves.

**Play Hangman.** This popular family game requires just a pencil and a scrap of paper, and it's a great diversion during endless waits in the doctor's office or a restaurant. When it's your turn to give a word, don't use the simplest word you can think of. Offer a more challenging choice, and explain the word once the child has guessed all the letters.

**Look It Up!** You're never too old to learn new words. Let your third grader see you looking up words whose meaning you're not sure about. It's a rare adult who doesn't occasionally come across a word she doesn't know. When you are stumped by a new word, mention to your child that you don't know the meaning of the word: "This article mentions the aorta. You know, I've never really understood where in the heart the aorta is. I'm going to look it up in the dictionary." Encourage your child to do the same thing when she meets a new word.

**Play *Balderdash*!** Commercial games like *Balderdash* and *Balderdash Jr.* are fun games that will build and enrich vocabulary. Start a family game night and introduce this game.

**Play Word Scramble.** This ever-popular party game can be lots of fun for children to play, especially if you get several children together and offer a prize for the most words. In word scramble, choose one larger word (such as *Halloween*), and have children find as many smaller words as they can using the same letters as are in the larger word. Set a time limit.

**Play Internet Wordfind.** If your child seems reluctant to use a dictionary, try the Internet. Dictionary skills are important, but your aim at this age is to get your child used to looking up words she doesn't know. Finding the meaning of a word using the "search" key isn't practicing dictionary skills, but it is a way for you to capture her interest in learning new words.

**Use Word-a-Day Calendars.** Try a junior version of the word-a-day calendars. It works!

## What Tests May Ask

Standardized tests for third graders assess vocabulary development in several ways. Most often, these tests look at how your child understands the meaning of words by using several types of questions. One type of question presents the word in isolation:

A <u>car</u> is something to

Ⓐ eat.

Ⓑ drive.

Ⓒ wear.

Ⓓ hold.

In a situation like this, if the child doesn't already know the word, she may have to guess because there aren't any other clues in the sentence to help her figure out the definition. Another type of question presents a word in a sentence, and asks for an interpretation. This could be done by presenting the word in a sentence and simply asking for its meaning:

The shirt he tried on was too <u>snug</u>. <u>Snug</u> means

Ⓐ tight.

Ⓑ ugly.

Ⓒ soft.

Ⓓ cute.

Or a test may give one sentence and ask the child to identify another sentence that uses the same word in a similar way:

I went to the sale and got a <u>free</u> book.

In which sentence does the word <u>free</u> mean the same thing it does as in the sentence above?

Ⓐ The lion cub was born <u>free</u>.

Ⓑ If I send in boxtops, I'll get the toy for <u>free</u>.

Ⓒ He tried to <u>free</u> the trapped bird.

Ⓓ Are you <u>free</u> for dinner tonight?

In order for your third grader to do well on this vocabulary section of a typical standardized test, she needs to know not just what a word means but also how it is used correctly in a sentence.

## Practice Skill: Vocabulary

**Directions:** Choose the correct word to go in the blank in these sentences.

**Example:**

The dog chased a ____.

Ⓐ ball

Ⓑ bone

Ⓒ hole

Ⓓ gass

**Answer:**

Ⓐ ball

1 The woman put her ____ in the washing machine.

Ⓐ clothes

Ⓑ stone

Ⓒ car

Ⓓ eraser

**2** I was afraid I had ____ my ring.

Ⓐ lose

Ⓑ fear

Ⓒ find

Ⓓ lost

**3** As the moon rose, we heard an ____ screech.

Ⓐ pig

Ⓑ worm

Ⓒ cow

Ⓓ owl

**4** Ellen was happy because her project was a _____.

Ⓐ failure

Ⓑ success

Ⓒ problem

Ⓓ good

**Directions:** Choose the answer that means the same as the underlined word.

**5** A fable is something that

Ⓐ carries a TV program.

Ⓑ teaches a lesson.

Ⓒ is used to make clothes.

Ⓓ you wear.

**6** If the writing is faint, it means it is

Ⓐ bright.

Ⓑ crooked.

Ⓒ dark.

Ⓓ light and unclear.

**7** A fawn is a

Ⓐ kind of dress.

Ⓑ baby deer.

Ⓒ baby cow.

Ⓓ type of cereal.

**Directions:** Choose the sentence below in which the underlined word means the same thing as in the sample sentence.

**Example:**

I need to get some air.

Ⓐ She needs to air her grievances.

Ⓑ The player had the air knocked out of him.

Ⓒ What time is the TV program going to air?

Ⓓ The actor did not know he was on the air.

**Answer:**

Ⓑ The player had the air knocked out of him.

**8** I want to <u>brush</u> my hair.

   Ⓐ  Jim picked up the <u>brush</u> from the table.

   Ⓑ  Jane is going to <u>brush</u> the horse's mane.

   Ⓒ  The fox ran off into the <u>brush</u>.

   Ⓓ  He was just going to <u>brush</u> past without saying hello!

**9** The black <u>bear</u> climbed up a tree.

   Ⓐ  We have the right to <u>bear</u> weapons.

   Ⓑ  Lee can't <u>bear</u> it!

   Ⓒ  The class will just have to <u>bear</u> the loss.

   Ⓓ  Emma likes to look at the <u>bear</u> in the zoo.

**10** Kara is going to <u>tear</u> up the contract.

   Ⓐ  Brittany saw a <u>tear</u> in her mother's eye.

   Ⓑ  Lolo the cat will <u>tear</u> up the curtains.

   Ⓒ  The lonely man shed a <u>tear</u> for his lost kitten.

   Ⓓ  Miranda could hardly <u>tear</u> her eyes away from the dog.

**Directions:** Choose the answer that means the same as the underlined word.

**11** Buster likes to read <u>fantasies</u>. <u>Fantasies</u> mean

   Ⓐ  factual stories that could happen in real life.

   Ⓑ  stories about peoples lives.

   Ⓒ  stories told in poetry form.

   Ⓓ  stories that have events or characters that couldn't exist in real life.

**12** Abraham Lincoln never told a <u>falsehood</u>. <u>Falsehood</u> means

   Ⓐ  lie.

   Ⓑ  funny story.

   Ⓒ  scary story.

   Ⓓ  story about clothing.

(See page 115 for answer key.)

## Analogies

An *analogy* is a relationship between a pair of words that serves as the basis of creating another pair with the same relationship to each other. An analogy is really a type of word puzzle, which some children find easy to do and others find more challenging. In any case, working on analogies gives students practice in analyzing relationships and strengthens their vocabulary.

Analogies are usually written in a specific form:

Happy is to sad as kind is to mean

Your child may find the analogy is shortened by the use of colons:

happy : sad : : kind : mean

## What Third Graders Should Know

Your child should be familiar with the basic structure of simple analogies and be able to fill in the blank in a straightforward example. You can expect that students will be studying analogies for many more years. Your child should be able to read the first pair of terms and think about the relationship between them; using this information, she should be able to complete the analogy without too much help.

## What Tests May Ask

Standardized tests almost always include some questions on analogies. In general, they will present the first pair of words, and the first word of the second pair, and ask the child to fill in the blank to complete the analogy from a list of four choices. Some tests may give the first pair of analogies and then ask students to choose the correct second pair of analogies from a group of choices.

In dealing with analogies, your child should first think about the first pair and decide what the relationship is between them. She might ask herself these questions: Are the first pair antonyms or synonyms? Are they homophones? Is one word a part of the other, or a member of the same group?

## Practice Skill: Analogies

**Directions:** Choose the word that best completes the analogy.

**Example:**

coconut : tree :: grape : _____

(A) raisin     (B) wine

(C) vine     (D) fruit

**Answer:**

(C) vine

13 eyes : see :: ears : _____

(A) hear     (B) sight

(C) noise     (D) nose

14 fruit : apple :: flower : _____

(A) blossom     (B) pollen

(C) pretty     (D) smell

15 beef: meat :: asparagus : _____

(A) fruit

(B) eat

(C) vegetable

(D) meet

16 wild : tame :: strong : _____

(A) powerful

(B) weak

(C) flame

(D) force

**Directions:** Choose the pair of terms that best completes the analogy.

**Example:**

shell : egg:: _____

Ⓐ orange : fruit

Ⓑ bird : nest

Ⓒ seed : apple

Ⓓ skin : peach

**Answer:**

Ⓓ skin : peach

17 read : book :: _____

Ⓐ listen : tape

Ⓑ music : concert

Ⓒ taste : sweet

Ⓓ book : newspaper

18 hair : head :: _____

Ⓐ hand : glove

Ⓑ bald : skin

Ⓒ cap : hat

Ⓓ nail : finger

(See page 115 for answer key.)

## CHAPTER 3

# Word Meanings in Context

When children first learn to read, they read each word separately, as if it existed alone without any relationship to words that came before or after it. As children become more sophisticated and experienced readers, however, they begin to read words as parts of sentences, in *context*. They probably don't even realize they are no longer focusing on each word individually but instead on the way words relate to each other within sentences. They will begin to appreciate the shades of word meanings within their existing vocabulary. They will also add new words at a faster pace because they will be able to decode the meaning of unfamiliar words based on the rest of the sentence.

## What Third Graders Should Know

Third-grade students are fluent readers who understand that the sentence as a whole should make sense. Third graders can read out loud with expression and cadence because they are reading words in their context. The ability to read words in context also means that when a third grader comes to a word he does not know, he should be able to puzzle out its meaning based on the surrounding words in the phrase or sentence. And each time this happens, he adds yet another word to his vocabulary. As his vocabulary grows, the third grader is able to read more and more difficult books, which expands his vocabulary even more.

## What You and Your Child Can Do

**Read!** Reading to your child—and having him read to you—will increase his vocabulary skills at an amazing rate. When he reads to you, if he comes to a word he doesn't understand, have him stop and see if he can puzzle it out from the context of the sentence. Let him see how the words within the sentence relate to each other.

**Have Fun with Sentences.** While you're waiting to be served in a restaurant, try to work on context this way: Give your child a sentence with a word missing. See how many words he can think of that would fit in the blank and still make sense. Talk about which ones seem most logical.

---

### READING TIP

**If your child stumbles over a word when reading out loud, have him go on to finish the sentence. Then have him go back to the word to see if he can figure out what it means.**

---

**What's This?** If your child asks you to define a word for him, don't automatically provide the definition. Instead, use the word in several sentences to see if he can work out the meaning on his own.

CHILD:     What does *bigot* mean?

PARENT:   Well, let's see. What do you think it means in this sentence: "Only a bigot would judge a person based on the color of his skin." Or "Only an intolerant bigot would refuse to hire someone of a different religion."

**Play Context Cross-out.** The next time you're in a restaurant that gives children take-home menus, try this game: Cross out every fifth or sixth word. See if your child can figure out what word you crossed out by looking at the context of the sentences. You can also try this activity with a children's magazine or catalog.

**Model It.** Let your child see you going back to reread a sentence or two if you don't understand a particular word. Your child needs to understand that this strategy is often used by experienced readers.

**Question Yourself.** Have your child ask himself "What would make sense?" when he comes to a word he doesn't understand.

**Try This.** A good way to work on the idea of context with your child is to read Lewis Carroll's wonderful nonsense poem "Jabberwocky" from *Through the Looking Glass.* It begins:

'Twas brillig and the slithy toves
Did gyre and gimbel through the wabe.
All mimsy were the borogroves
And the mome raths outgrabe.

Discuss the meaning of this poem, and help your child to see how he could somehow figure out a meaning despite all the crazy words. Help him write his own nonsense poem.

## What Tests May Ask

Most standardized tests will assess your child's ability to understand the meaning of words as they are used in particular contexts. The tests will offer a sentence and ask the child to fill in the blank with the word that makes the most sense. This requires a child to understand what words do and do not fit into a sentence given a sentence's meaning and also requires that he

understand that a word may have more than one meaning.

## Practice Skill: Word Meanings in Context

**Directions:** Read each passage. For each blank, choose the word that best fits in the sentence.

**Example:**

It was time to go to school. Sarah ran out the ___1___ and climbed into the ___2___.

1   (A) bed          2   (A) bike
    (B) door             (B) cake
    (C) window           (C) bucket
    (D) bun              (D) bus

**Answer:**

1 (B) door    2 (D) bus

*The Wizard of Oz* was written by L. Frank Baum. He used to tell ___1___ to his children and their ___2___. His story about Oz is about the ___3___ of Dorothy, a ___4___ from Kansas.

1   (A) tunes
    (B) lies
    (C) stories
    (D) books

2   (A) friends
    (B) dogs
    (C) monkeys
    (D) toys

3  Ⓐ  manners
   Ⓑ  ideas
   Ⓒ  adventures
   Ⓓ  balloons

4  Ⓐ  governess
   Ⓑ  witch
   Ⓒ  girl
   Ⓓ  boy

**Directions:** Read the statements below. Choose the word that means the **opposite** of the underlined word.

**Example:**

at the <u>back</u> of the house
   Ⓐ  rear
   Ⓑ  middle
   Ⓒ  side
   Ⓓ  front

**Answer:**

   Ⓓ  front

5  We must <u>stop</u> the music.
   Ⓐ  play
   Ⓑ  start
   Ⓒ  hear
   Ⓓ  end

6  at the <u>top</u> of the class
   Ⓐ  bottom
   Ⓑ  middle
   Ⓒ  rear
   Ⓓ  tip

**Directions:** Read each sentence. Choose the correct word to fill in the blank.

**Example:**

Marcy wrapped her puppy's foot in a _____ to stop the bleeding.
   Ⓐ  purse
   Ⓑ  tourniquet
   Ⓒ  ribbon
   Ⓓ  book

**Answer:**

   Ⓑ  tourniquet

7  Kristi and Lee tried to _____ the old woman who was shivering with cold.
   Ⓐ  cool
   Ⓑ  wonder
   Ⓒ  comfort
   Ⓓ  work

8  Brittany will have to _____ the price of the candy since it cost so much to make.
   Ⓐ  increase
   Ⓑ  eat
   Ⓒ  lose
   Ⓓ  lower

9  The _____ of wind blew the enormous tree down in the storm.
   Ⓐ  trickle
   Ⓑ  gust
   Ⓒ  burp
   Ⓓ  whisper

**10** Becca will have to _____ again because she lost her place in the music.

   Ⓐ  begin

   Ⓑ  sleep

   Ⓒ  move

   Ⓓ  soft

**11** The kitten whimpered because she was in _____.

   Ⓐ  town

   Ⓑ  giggles

   Ⓒ  laughing

   Ⓓ  pain

**Directions:** In the following examples, read each sentence and choose the answer that means the same as the underlined word.

**Example:**

The boy seldom looked before he <u>leaped</u>.

   Ⓐ  ran

   Ⓑ  jumped

   Ⓒ  parked

   Ⓓ  swam

**Answer:**

   Ⓑ  jumped

**12** Elizabeth will <u>proceed</u> with the project.

   Ⓐ  never

   Ⓑ  seldom

   Ⓒ  frequently

   Ⓓ  continue

**13** It's <u>likely</u> that Mrs. Taylor will give the class a test tomorrow.

   Ⓐ  happily

   Ⓑ  probable

   Ⓒ  slowly

   Ⓓ  quickly

**14** John was <u>satisfied</u> with his drawing of the truck.

   Ⓐ  unhappy

   Ⓑ  angry

   Ⓒ  giggly

   Ⓓ  content

**15** The chipmunks will <u>hoard</u> nuts for the winter.

   Ⓐ  throw away

   Ⓑ  stash

   Ⓒ  hit

   Ⓓ  throw

(See page 115 for answer key.)

## CHAPTER 4

# Antonyms, Synonyms, and Homophones

If your child is to be a good reader and an eloquent writer, she must fully understand the basis of her language—which she learns mostly at home. You may be surprised to know just how much learning does go on at home—and the more informal and less like school the home environment is, the better.

A *synonym* is a word that sounds different from but means "the same as" another word. *Hurried* and *dashed* are typical examples of synonyms that third graders will be able to understand. An *antonym* is a word that is the opposite of another word, such as *started* versus *finished*. A *homophone* is a word that sounds like another word but has a different meaning and/or spelling, such as *brake* versus *break*.

Because a basic understanding of "alike" and "different" is vital to being a good reader, you can bet these concepts will be included on most standardized tests.

## Antonyms and Synonyms

### What Third Graders Should Know

By third grade your child has developed a solid understanding of word meanings. She understands that words have opposites and similarities, and she knows the terms *antonym* and *synonym*. She can recognize both types of words in the context of what she reads.

By this age, your child should have begun to develop language that is both rich and complex. A necklace is not just pretty but may be sparkling, gorgeous, wonderful. A friend might smile happily or sadly, brightly, or wisely. This flexibility in language now extends to the idea of one-way relationships—for example, while all spaniels are dogs, not all dogs are spaniels.

## What You and Your Child Can Do

**FLASH!** Have your child design a new synonym flash card each day. First, she identifies an unfamiliar term in the dictionary, which she jots down on a card. Then she writes on the card any synonyms or antonyms she can find for the new word. On the front of the card, she can draw an image based on the new word. For example, to illustrate *gigantic,* your child might draw a whale beside a tiny boat to show the scale.

Over dinner, have your child show the picture on the front of the index card; everyone has three chances to guess the new vocabulary word. Once the term is revealed, take turns seeing who can suggest synonyms and antonyms. The person with the most synonyms or antonyms wins.

**Synonym Card Game.** This is a simple synonym matching game you can make yourself. First, take a pack of index cards, and write down one common word on each card. On a second set of index cards (contrasting colors work well), write less-common synonyms for the common words. You can laminate the cards to make them last if you wish, storing them in a plastic bag.

To play, spread the common words on a table or desk so that all the cards can easily be seen. Shuffle the less-common cards. Take turns drawing one card and match the words on the synonym cards to the common word for which they are a synonym.

To get you started, try these common words and their synonyms:

LAUGH: chortle, chuckle, grin, cackle, hoot, giggle, snicker

CRY: whimper, wail, howl, weep, moan, whine, sob

HAPPY: thrilled, delighted, blissful, jovial

SAD: forlorn, miserable, wretched, dejected, disheartened, depressed

WALK: saunter, shuffle, plod, trudge, step, stroll

RUN: dash, dart, race, scramble, chase, bolt, trot, scoot

**Time for Synonyms and Antonyms.** In this game, set a timer for two minutes and have players write down a list of as many antonyms (or synonyms) as they can. The player with the most words at the end of the two minutes is the winner.

## What Tests May Ask

Standardized tests for third graders will assess a child's understanding of similarities and opposites in several ways. Test questions may ask youngsters to choose a synonym or antonym for the underlined word in a sentence from among a group of possibilities, or the test may present groups of two words and ask your child to choose the pair of words that mean the same thing.

Then your child may be asked to choose from a given list a pair of words in which the words do **not** mean the same thing.

All these variations on the synonym and antonym theme are ways to ensure that your child understands that it's possible for two different words to carry the same—or the opposite—meanings.

If your child has a good vocabulary and you've raised her to love language and reading, she shouldn't have a problem with antonyms and synonyms on standardized tests.

## Practice Skill: Synonyms

**Directions:** Read each item and choose the word that means the same as the underlined word.

**Example:**

Jane was <u>angry</u> about losing the game.

Ⓐ furious

Ⓑ happy

Ⓒ hungry

Ⓓ pleased

**Answer:**

Ⓐ furious

---

1 Sam <u>often</u> sleeps late on Saturdays.

Ⓐ rarely

Ⓑ occasionally

Ⓒ frequently

Ⓓ never

---

**2** The clown <u>smiled</u> at the monkey.

    Ⓐ shouted

    Ⓑ sobbed

    Ⓒ growled

    Ⓓ grinned

**3** The woods were <u>quiet</u>.

    Ⓐ very

    Ⓑ silent

    Ⓒ loud

    Ⓓ dark

**4** The cow slowly <u>walked</u> into the barn.

    Ⓐ sauntered

    Ⓑ ran

    Ⓒ galloped

    Ⓓ mooed

**Directions:** Choose the pair of synonyms from the word pairs listed below.

**Example:**

    Ⓐ run    walk

    Ⓑ spin    turn

    Ⓒ fly    flea

    Ⓓ see    sea

**Answer:**

    Ⓑ spin    turn

**5** Ⓐ be    bee

    Ⓑ dash    run

    Ⓒ sit    stand

    Ⓓ break    brake

**6** Ⓐ hair    heir

    Ⓑ go    come

    Ⓒ jump    hop

    Ⓓ think    thought

**7** Ⓐ throw    pitch

    Ⓑ brush    brush

    Ⓒ sink    swim

    Ⓓ die    dye

**Directions:** Choose the pair of words from the lists below that is **not** a pair of synonyms.

**Example:**

    Ⓐ run    walk

    Ⓑ spin    turn

    Ⓒ fly    soar

    Ⓓ see    spy

**Answer:**

    Ⓐ run    walk

**8** Ⓐ sick    ill

    Ⓑ flower    blossom

    Ⓒ best    worst

    Ⓓ happy    glad

9  (A)  thin        skinny
   (B)  speedy      fast
   (C)  story       tale
   (D)  tall        short

10 (A)  seldom      rarely
   (B)  pretty      lovely
   (C)  found       lost
   (D)  skip        hop

(See page 115 for answer key.)

## Practice Skill: Antonyms

**Directions:** Read each item and choose the word that is an antonym of the underlined word.

**Example:**

Emma was <u>angry</u> about losing the game.

(A)  furious
(B)  happy
(C)  hungry
(D)  sad

**Answer:**

(B)  happy

11  The dress was very <u>pretty</u>.
    (A)  ugly
    (B)  attractive
    (C)  beautiful
    (D)  blue

12  Kara was a <u>strong</u> swimmer.
    (A)  good
    (B)  tall
    (C)  pretty
    (D)  weak

13  Bill was a <u>good</u> painter.
    (A)  bad
    (B)  wild
    (C)  mean
    (D)  silly

14  Rachel owned a very <u>smart</u> horse.
    (A)  clever
    (B)  intelligent
    (C)  wily
    (D)  dumb

**Directions:** Choose the pair of antonyms from the word pairs listed below.

**Example:**

(A)  run        walk
(B)  spin       turn
(C)  fly        flea
(D)  see        sea

**Answer:**

(A)  run        walk

15
(A) top        high
(B) party      fun
(C) sit        stand
(D) train      train

16
(A) eat        ate
(B) star       star
(C) tall       high
(D) hairy      bald

17
(A) old        ancient
(B) cool       chilly
(C) hot        cold
(D) sore       soar

18
(A) lie        lye
(B) oar        are
(C) seldom     often
(D) collection group

19
(A) noise      sound
(B) funny      sad
(C) remember   forget
(D) new        old

20
(A) dull       shine
(B) cuts       snips
(C) some       none
(D) asleep     awake

21
(A) go         come
(B) learn      forget
(C) clean      dirty
(D) let        allow

(See page 115 for answer key.)

**Directions:** Choose the pair of words from the lists below that is **not** a pair of antonyms.

**Example:**

(A) run        walk
(B) spin       turn
(C) fly        fall
(D) see        hide

**Answer:**

(B) spin       turn

## Homophones

Homophones can be tricky for children to spell, but it's well worth their time to do so. To master these words, children have to learn which spelling is connected to which meaning. As they incorporate these words into their vocabularies, they will need to visualize the words in addition to hearing them spoken. The extra effort notwithstanding, most children love working with homophones.

The terms *homophone* and *homonym* are often used interchangeably, but technically they refer to different types of words. *Homophones* are words that sound the same but have different meanings and/or different spellings (such as *bare* and *bear*).

*Homonyms* are both spelled the same and sound the same, but they have different meanings. For example, *drink* can be a verb ("Drink your milk!") or a noun ("I want a drink"). All homonyms are also homophones, but not all homophones are homonyms.

## What Third Graders Should Know

You may find that your child is at first still inflexible when faced with homophones and she may have trouble understanding the different meanings, but by the end of third grade she will probably be able to understand the subtleties of multimeaning words.

## What You and Your Child Can Do

**Be a News Hound.** As you read the daily paper, be on the lookout for an article that is appropriate for your child. Have her look for as many homophones in the article as she can find. You may want to start her off by circling or highlighting an example.

**Go on a Scavenger Hunt.** Send two children around your home on a homonym scavenger hunt, searching for items whose names have more than one meaning: the *batter* in your bowl and a *batter* in a baseball game; the *jar* on your shelf and the verb *jar* meaning "to startle." Have the children make a list of these words and see how long the list can get.

**Write a Story.** The best-known series of children's books featuring homophones is *Amelia Bedelia*. Your child may already have read one of these books, but if not, be sure to get one. Ask your child to write a paragraph or two with a main character like Amelia, using at least three homophones.

## Practice Skill: Homophones

**Directions:** Choose the correct word to complete the sentence.

**Example:**

Charmayne and Jill want _____ baseballs.

- Ⓐ there
- Ⓑ thair
- Ⓒ their
- Ⓓ they

Answer:

- Ⓒ their

---

**22** John heard that there is a black _____ in the forest.

- Ⓐ bare
- Ⓑ beir
- Ⓒ bear
- Ⓓ bar

---

**23** The veterinarian is going to _____ my pet dog.

- Ⓐ way
- Ⓑ weigh
- Ⓒ whey
- Ⓓ waye

---

**24** Jorge is going to the barber to get his _____ cut.

- Ⓐ hair
- Ⓑ hare
- Ⓒ heir
- Ⓓ air

---

**25** My mother does not want me to
_____ her favorite bowl.

- Ⓐ brake
- Ⓑ break
- Ⓒ brak
- Ⓓ brakie

**26** Do you want to go to the county
_____?

- Ⓐ fare
- Ⓑ fair
- Ⓒ fear
- Ⓓ feir

**27** I want to come, _____.

- Ⓐ to
- Ⓑ two
- Ⓒ too
- Ⓓ tu

(See page 115 for answer key.)

## CHAPTER 5

# Word Sounds

Word sounds continue to be an important part of the third-grade curriculum in most schools. The study of word sounds includes vowel sounds, consonant blends and digraphs, and both beginning and ending consonant sounds.

Your child needs to know how to separate, manipulate, and identify sounds within words if he is going to be a good reader. Understanding the structure of words is another important part of word analysis that will boost reading comprehension as he progresses in school.

## Consonant Sounds

The study of consonant sounds includes both beginning and ending consonant sounds (such as the S in Sun or the ending S in catS). A *consonant blend* is the sound created when two or three consonants together are heard either at the beginning or ending of a word:

    GRoup    or    STRike

    deSK     or    teST

A *consonant digraph* is the sound created when two consonants together are heard as one sound: WH, CH, SH, and TH.

## What Third Graders Should Know

Most second graders are quite skilled at picking out consonant digraphs such as CH or WH. As children enter third grade, they should be able to recognize single and multiple consonant sounds at the beginning and ending of words. Most new third graders are accurate in detecting single-consonant endings (such as haT) and both beginning and ending consonant blends (like siNG). Throughout third grade, children continue to develop their ability to identify word sounds.

In addition to knowing what sound letters make, your child should be able to hear and manipulate sounds within words, and he should be able to identify words that rhyme. These would include words that have the same ending sound even though they may not have the same spelling: wood, hood, could, should. He also should understand the basics of prefixes, suffixes, and word roots.

## What You and Your Child Can Do

**Dessert Digraphs.** Here's an activity that's sure to please any third grader. Since one of the most common digraphs (CH) is the beginning for the word *chocolate,* try working on digraphs on make-your-own-sundae night at your house. As you sit around the table trying out toppings, point out how many digraphs are contained in these delicious desserts. Challenge your child to see how many he can come up with. Does he like CHocolate, with WHipped cream and a CHerry? How about CHopped walnuts? You'll be amazed at how many you can come up with.

**Guessing Game.** During a long car ride, play the "I'm thinking of" game: "I'm thinking of a word that starts with the hard C sound (Cat) or hard G (Got), or a soft C (Celery) or soft G (Gym)."

**Word Sound Card Game.** Get a pack of multi-colored index cards. With a marker, print two cards each of these common consonants: B, C, D, G, K, L, M, P, R, S, and T (all the same color). Then make another set using different color index cards printing these common letter patterns:

AN, AT, EN, ET, IN, ING, IT, OP, OT, UG, UST

Put the consonant cards face down in the middle of the table. Next, deal five of the letter pattern cards to each player. Each player draws a consonant card from the pile on the table and tries to make a word using any of the letter pattern cards in his hand (such as R + OT or T + AN). Any matches are laid down on the table in front of the player, who says the word out loud. If a player makes a word, his turn continues and he can draw another consonant from the pile. If he can make still another match, he lays that one down. He may continue to play until he can't make a match. If he can't match the consonant with any word pattern in his hand, he puts the consonant card back on the bottom of the deck, and play continues to his left.

**Computer Games.** To help your child sound out words, try *Kid Phonics 2* (Davidson & Associates), designed for children aged six through nine; *Schoolhouse Rock* (Creative Wonders); *Word Munchers Deluxe* (MECC/Softkey); and *Phonics Alive* and *Phonics Alive 2* (Scholastic).

**Consonant Concentration.** In this game, you can focus on *cluster consonants*—those consonants that appear in triplicate (such as SCReam or SPLash). Make a list of as many words with cluster consonants as you can. When you've got an even number (12 is good), write them down twice on individual index cards. Cut each index card in half so that you have 24 cards with one word each. Turn them face down and play as you would regular concentration: Each player turns over two cards. If they match, the player "wins" those cards and takes another turn. The player with the most cards at the end of the game wins.

## What Tests May Ask

The word analysis section of a typical standardized test will try to determine how well your child can separate and identify word sounds and the letters that make up those sounds. Tests may also assess how well he can understand the composition of words. You can learn more specifics about what tests will ask in the sections below.

Standardized tests will include questions on both beginning and ending consonant sounds. They will ask your child to hear and identify similarities in word sounds: Which word begins with the same sound as *give*?

jail     gym     got

Questions may attempt to distract the child with similar sounds, which might have tripped up younger students. By third grade, however, students should be able to identify beginning and ending sounds, which will enable them to choose the correct answer from similar-sounding choices.

## Practice Skill: Beginning Word Sounds

**Directions:** Choose the pair of words in which both words **begin** with the same sound.

**Example:**

- (A)  ball        fall
- (B)  lank        hank
- (C)  car         kind
- (D)  gotten      gyp

**Answer:**

- (C)  car         kind

---

1  (A)  chill       call
   (B)  think       toad
   (C)  catnip      king
   (D)  jell        golly

---

2  (A)  jewel       jam
   (B)  canter      church
   (C)  glove       giant
   (D)  cake        church

---

3  (A)  dunce       once
   (B)  circuit     cardboard
   (C)  shoot       shine
   (D)  chug        candy

---

**Directions:** Choose the word with the same **beginning** sound as the under-lined word in the question.

4  Choose the word below that has the same **beginning** sound as brain.

- (A)  bean
- (B)  bridge
- (C)  bald
- (D)  bituminous

5  Choose the word below with the same **beginning** sound as kitchen.

- (A)  candy
- (B)  chime
- (C)  charity
- (D)  go

---

(See page 115 for answer key.)

## Practice Skill: Ending Word Sounds

**Directions:** Choose the word with the same **ending** sound as the underlined word in the question.

**Example:** Which of these words has the same **ending** sound as the word hearth?

- (A)  deal
- (B)  hear
- (C)  seat
- (D)  heath

**Answer:**

- (D)  heath

---

6  Which of these words has the same **ending** sound as poach?

- (A)  punt
- (B)  pear
- (C)  filch
- (D)  think

---

**7** Which of these words has the same **ending** sound as <u>beach</u>?

(A) fit

(B) peach

(C) ball

(D) bite

---

**8** Which of these words has the same **ending** sound as <u>bass</u>?

(A) faith

(B) bat

(C) batch

(D) dogs

---

**9** Which of these words has the same **ending** sound as <u>seat</u>?

(A) start

(B) steer

(C) tease

(D) church

---

(See page 115 for answer key.)

## Consonant Blends

When two or more consonants are beside each other, sometimes the consonant sounds "blend" together, although each sound is heard. For example, in the word *black,* you hear the B, but you also hear the L—because the two consonants are next to each other.

## What Third Graders Should Know

By third grade, your child will understand consonant blends—that two consonants together blend together but each sound is heard separately. Your child should be able to identify these blends in speaking and reading.

## What You and Your Child Can Do

**Sentence Salad.** In this activity, you can help teach your child consonant blends. First, sit down with your child and think up consonant blends for nouns, verbs, and adjectives. Take a stack of index cards, and print one word on each card. Place the cards face down in three piles (nouns, verbs, and adjectives). Have your child choose one card from each pile and create a sentence using these words.

**Tongue Twisters.** Here's a fun way to practice consonant blends. Have your child make up a tongue twister using consonant blends of all one kind. For example, for the consonant blend ST you could try: Stark stones are standing still in the stable stalls.

**Guessing Game.** Another consonant game that can be adapted to teaching blends is the guessing game: "I'm thinking of a word that starts with the blend ST (Stone)."

**Timed End Blends.** Players gather around a stack of face-down index cards that have been marked with ending consonant blends, such as SK, NT, ST, MP, and FT. One card is drawn. Set a timer for one or two minutes (or more, depending on players' ages), and during that time players write down as many words that end in the consonant blend as they can. When the timer sounds, players draw the next card and play continues. The winner is the player with the most words overall.

## What Tests May Ask

Standardized tests will include questions on consonant blends, including some questions that may attempt to distract a child with similar sounds. Third graders should be able to identify consonant blends correctly from similar-sounding choices.

# Practice Skill: Consonant Blends

**Directions:** Choose the letter blend that makes the beginning sound for the word in the question.

**Example:**

tree

- Ⓐ T
- Ⓑ TR
- Ⓒ TRE
- Ⓓ TCH

**Answer:**

- Ⓑ TR

---

**10** sharp

- Ⓐ CH
- Ⓑ S
- Ⓒ SP
- Ⓓ SH

---

**11** slapstick

- Ⓐ S
- Ⓑ SP
- Ⓒ ST
- Ⓓ SL

---

**12** white

- Ⓐ WH
- Ⓑ W
- Ⓒ WE
- Ⓓ H

---

**13** grovel

- Ⓐ G
- Ⓑ R
- Ⓒ GE
- Ⓓ GR

---

**Directions:** Choose the letter blend that makes the ending sound for the word given in each question.

**Example:**

lump

- Ⓐ MP
- Ⓑ NP
- Ⓒ P
- Ⓓ ST

**Answer:**

- Ⓐ MP

---

**14** first

- Ⓐ T
- Ⓑ SP
- Ⓒ ST
- Ⓓ SL

---

**15** whisk

- Ⓐ CH
- Ⓑ CK
- Ⓒ K
- Ⓓ SK

---

**16** finest

    (A) ST

    (B) S

    (C) T

    (D) SH

(See page 115 for answer key.)

## Vowel Sounds

English is a language with complicated and sometimes unpredictable rules for vowel sounds that can stump many children. However, the parts of the brain that govern sophisticated vowel sounds have developed so that the brain structures are in place to allow most third graders to easily handle lessons in vowels.

## What Third Graders Should Know

While early readers may not see much point in vowels, by third grade children will know what vowels are and will be able to identify basic vowel sounds such as "the vowels that say their name" (as the A sound in Ate), different sounds made by the same vowels (such as the O sound in hOp and bOth), and sounds made by vowel combinations such as the OA in bOAr, the EA in tEAm, and so on. They should also understand some of the irregular vowels like AL, AW, and AU, in addition to words with same vowel sounds (fAWn and sAUce).

## What You and Your Child Can Do

**Hangman.** This old favorite is good for building a wide variety of verbal skills, including learning vowels. Explain to your child that all words must have vowels and that means that a good way to begin guessing the letters for a word in hangman is to begin with each vowel: A, E, I, O, and U. As your child becomes more sophisticat-

ed with word play, he will see that in English, certain vowels are more likely to occur in some combinations than others or in some locations in a word more than in others (that is, most words will have a vowel as the second or third letter).

**Guess the Word.** In this game, you try to get your child to guess the vowel sound:

PARENT:  I'm thinking of a three-letter word that means an animal, and it has the vowel A that says its name.

CHILD:  Cat!

## What Tests May Ask

Standardized tests will include questions on vowel sounds, and they may include distracting questions with similar sounds. By third grade, your child should have sufficient experience in identifying vowel sounds that he can confidently pick the correct answer from similar-sounding choices.

## Practice Skill: Vowel Sounds

**Directions:** Choose the word with the same vowel sound as the given word in each question.

**Example:**

Which word has the same **vowel** sound as the word <u>toast</u>?

    (A) booth

    (B) rode

    (C) tap

    (D) hop

**Answer:**

    (B) rode

**17** What word has the same **vowel** sound as the word <u>hat</u>?

Ⓐ hop

Ⓑ had

Ⓒ head

Ⓓ hip

**18** Which word has the same **vowel** sound as the word <u>bright</u>?

Ⓐ star

Ⓑ tight

Ⓒ coal

Ⓓ fat

**19** Which word has the same **vowel** sound as the word <u>cook</u>?

Ⓐ fought

Ⓑ school

Ⓒ book

Ⓓ cake

**20** Which word has the same **vowel** sound as the word <u>cream</u>?

Ⓐ taught

Ⓑ tight

Ⓒ mat

Ⓓ mcct

(See page 115 for answer key.)

## CHAPTER 6

# Spelling

In the adult world, people are often judged by the correct or incorrect spelling in their written work. Even in today's world of spellcheckers and grammar checkers, a person's ability to spell correctly is very important. Every spelling error in a written document diminishes the writer's credibility a little bit. In the other direction, a spelling-error-free document conveys an image of a competent writer.

Almost all schools use some type of basic word list of common words that students are expected to master. Ask your child's teacher what list she uses, and see if you can get a copy so that you will know what words your child is learning at school.

Ask your child's teacher for a copy of your state's third-grade word list. If your teacher can't provide one, you can write to the instructional division of your state department of public instruction and ask whether there is a list and if there is, will they send you a copy.

## Spelling

### What Third Graders Should Know

By third grade your child should be spelling both common and irregular words with ease. When your child hears the word *key,* she should be able to predict that the first letter is either a *c* or *k* and that the rest of the word will be made with an *e* followed by *y.* Your child also should be ready to learn common spelling rules, such as "*i* before *e,* except after *c*" and "change the *y* to *i*

and add *es* (as in *cities*). By this age, your third grader should be using multisyllable and irregularly spelled words in her daily writing.

Most third graders also should be able to find spelling errors, which is a more complicated skill than simply memorizing spelling words. At this age, your child should be able to check her writing and flag words for which she's not sure of the spelling so that she can look them up in the dictionary.

## What You and Your Child Can Do

Spelling doesn't have to be drudgery—there are plenty of ways you can make spelling practice fun. When working on spelling, however, it's best to use games that will allow your child to write the words. People don't spell out loud, except in artificial situations. Because we usually write or read words, children need to develop a visual image of words so that they can learn when a word "looks right." This is one reason that spelling bees aren't the best way to practice spelling.

**Play Hangman.** This old favorite is a wonderful way to learn spelling words. Have your child choose a word, and mark out the spaces for each letter. Then you guess what the word is. Switch roles, and you choose a word and let your child guess what it is. Give your child some helpful strategies: Suggest she try vowels first since all words must have vowels. Ask her which letters are most common. If the second letter is an *h,* talk about what letter might go with the *h—s* or *c,* for example. You can play this game anywhere, with paper and pencil, on a chalkboard, dry erase board—even with magnetic letters on a fridge. If your child is computer savvy, she can play hangman online at the Web site nanana.com/hngmn.htm. Log on and have fun with this interactive game.

**Play with Magnetic Letters.** Let your child spell her weekly words on the fridge while you cook.

**Look It Up.** Get your child an inexpensive, age-appropriate dictionary, and encourage her to check the spelling of words.

**Be an Editor!** By third grade, children should be used to the process of editing. When your third grader writes a note to Aunt Barbara to thank her for the scooter, have her write a rough draft and then check it with her for major errors. Some words are just too difficult to sound out and spell correctly. If you detect a misspelled word, see if she can come up with the correct spelling. Then look it up together in the dictionary.

**Use Sensory Spelling.** The more senses your child uses when learning, the better she'll remember. Try tracing a word on your child's back and have her say the word. This is a good game to play with friends during a sleepover. Or cover a washable surface with shaving cream for tracing spelling words. Try tracing words on fine sandpaper. A musical child might want to spell the letters by playing notes on a piano keyboard. At this age, you can try some supervised kitchen fun. Let her pour pancake batter in the shape of her spelling words, or cut them out of bread or soft American cheese.

**Play Concentration.** Take 15 words from your child's word list at school. Using a set of index cards, have your child print a word on each card. Print a second set and then turn all the cards over. The first player turns over two cards. If they match, she keeps the cards. If they don't

match, she puts them back where she got them. Repeat with the second player. As your child becomes more adept at playing, increase the number of spelling words to 20.

**Check Homework.** Use the same strategy with homework. Go over your child's written homework and point out misspellings. It's important that by this age you help your child get used to having written work edited. As you edit your child's homework and school papers she brings home, make a list of words your child routinely misspells. You'll find your child will routinely misspell the same words and make the same errors (usually one or two letters) in each difficult word. Make note cards with those words, with the routinely misspelled letters in a bold color. Drill her on the challenging words from time to time. For example, if she routinely misspells the word *school* as "skool," write it on the note card as "s**ch**ool."

**Obtain Spelling Lists.** Most state departments of public instruction provide lists of required (or recommended) words that children at each grade level should be able to read and spell. These lists can be a helpful resource because they are generally designed to match the vocabulary children encounter in each grade in the curriculum and the level of vocabulary tested in the standardized tests each state uses. Get this list from your teacher, your principal, or the state education department so that you will know the words your child should be able to spell.

**Eat Your Letters.** Ancient Hebrew mothers taught their children to spell by shaping letters out of cookie dough. The children would then hold the letter, say the sound, and then eat the letter. Try baking some letters and letting your child spell simple words—and then eat the results! You can find premixed sugar cookie dough in the refrigerator section of most grocery stores. Alpha Bits cereal is also good for this activity.

**Make a Word Pyramid.** In this game, you're trying to see how many words your child can make out of one beginning word. Start her off with a simple word, such as "ME." Have her print "ME" on a piece of paper or draw it on a chalkboard. Under it, add one more letter to make a word. Under each layer of the pyramid, add one more letter:

ME

MET

MEAT

STEAM

STEAMS

**Obtain Spelling Software.** Look for grade-appropriate software, such as *Spelling Blaster.* These programs provide immediate feedback and have the added advantage of presenting spelling in a nonthreatening, fun video game format that most children enjoy. If your child wants to use the family computer, visit the school and check out their software so that you can obtain it if possible.

If your third grader enjoys using your word processing software, turn on automatic spell flagging to help provide immediate feedback. New adult-level word processing software provides alerts such as alarm buzzers, flashing red underlines, or other ways of emphasizing misspelled words. Although these programs will flag words that they simply don't recognize (such as proper names), they will also flag misspellings. Thus when the child writes "I road the *buse* to school," she will see immediately that she has misspelled *bus.* (But note that they would typically not flag the incorrect spelling "road" because that is a correct spelling in another context.)

**Play Scrabblin' Spell.** You can use regular *Scrabble* tiles for this activity, or you can make your own letter tiles by simply cutting out squares from an index card and printing one let-ter in each square. Mix them up face down, and have your child pick six letters at random. Challenge her to see how many words she can spell. Foam sheets are also good for making tiles, and they are easier to handle. Trace the letters and cut them out with a sharp blade.

## What Tests May Ask

Standardized spelling tests can't ask your child to write down spelling words; instead, they will ask her to choose the correctly spelled word from a list of incorrect choices, or choose the one incorrect word from a list of possibilities. Tests will typically include difficult words that require a child to recognize the irregular use of spelling sounds, such as *sch* in *school.*

## Practice Skill: Spelling

**Directions:** Choose the correctly spelled word to go into the blank.

**Example:**

Susan wants _____ pie.

Ⓐ sum

Ⓑ sume

Ⓒ som

Ⓓ some

**Answer:**

Ⓓ some

1 I could barely hear her _____.

Ⓐ wisper

Ⓑ whisper

Ⓒ whispur

Ⓓ wizper

**2** The cake batter was _____.

   Ⓐ lumby

   Ⓑ lumpie

   Ⓒ lumpey

   Ⓓ lumpy

**3** This test is too _____.

   Ⓐ confusing

   Ⓑ confuzing

   Ⓒ confussing

   Ⓓ condfusing

**4** The salad dressing is too _____.

   Ⓐ cremey

   Ⓑ creamy

   Ⓒ creamie

   Ⓓ cremy

**Directions:** Pick out the word that is spelled **incorrectly** in the sentences below.

**Example:**

Are you going to wear the blak dress?

   Ⓐ you

   Ⓑ wear

   Ⓒ dress

   Ⓓ blak

**Answer:**

   Ⓓ blak

**5** The soldier faced his enemey.

   Ⓐ soldier

   Ⓑ faced

   Ⓒ his

   Ⓓ enemey

**6** The scarey character in this book was spooky.

   Ⓐ scarey

   Ⓑ character

   Ⓒ book

   Ⓓ spooky

**7** Did you see the dinosor exhibit at the museum?

   Ⓐ see

   Ⓑ dinosor

   Ⓒ exhibit

   Ⓓ museum

(See page 115 for answer key.)

## Root Words, Prefixes, and Suffixes

The problem with English words is that they don't stay the same. Verbs have endings: think, think*s*, think*ing*. We add prefixes and suffixes: *re*think, *in*suffer*able*.

*Root words* are the original forms of words that can be made into other words by adding a prefix or suffix. For example, the root word in *ugliest* is *ugly*. *Prefixes* are added at the beginning of words. Learning the meaning of prefixes can help third graders puzzle out the meaning of a word: *Pre-* means "before"; then *prewriting* may be "what you do before you write." *Suffixes* are word endings, such as the *-er* in *player*, and knowing the meaning of suffixes also can help a child understand, or *decode*, a word's meaning.

## What Third Graders Should Know

Most third graders know the term *root word* and understand the concept of prefixes and suffixes, which were introduced in second grade. Third graders should be learning the common prefixes such as:

- *dis-* (not)
- *un-* (not)
- *mis-* (not right)
- *re-* (do again)
- *de-* (from)
- *ex-* (out of or from)

Third graders should also know the common suffixes:

- *-ful* (full of)
- *-ness* (a condition of)
- *-less* (without)
- *-ly* (in a specified manner)
- *-y* (characterized by)
- *-en* (caused to be)
- *-able* (capable of)

## What You and Your Child Can Do

**Suffix Pantomime.** Using the suffixes *-ful* and *-ly*, make a list of common words on index cards: *cheer, play, slow, friend, loud, wild, pain,* and so on. Each player draws one of these cards in turn, adds one of the two possible endings and acts out the new word.

**Mix and Match.** To help your child work on root words, prefixes, and suffixes, print some common words on index cards, with separate endings. Lay out the cards, and have your child play "mix and match" with different beginnings and endings.

**Concentration.** In this version of concentration, you can take the index cards (root words, beginnings, and endings) you made in the activity above, and turn them face down. Have your child turn over two cards at a time; if the root word fits with a beginning or an ending, that's a match! Your child takes the cards and chooses again. At the end of the game, the player with the most matches wins.

**Scrabble Tips.** When you get out that *Scrabble* board, show your child how valuable a prefix or suffix can be. If the word *peat* is on the board, you can show your child how to add the prefix *re-* for a longer word. You can turn others into higher scores: Add an *-s* or *-ing* to *play,* or an *un-* to *happiness.* Offer your child an extra 5 points every time she uses a prefix or suffix in the game.

## What Tests May Ask

You can be sure that standardized tests for the third grade will include questions on root words, prefixes, and suffixes. In some cases, students will be asked to identify the root word, prefix, or suffix from a group of given words. Some questions will be straightforward, such as asking for the root word of *playing.* Other questions, however, may be more difficult, such as asking for the root word of *housing,* which would require that the student know that the *e* has been dropped from *house.*

## Practice Skill: Root Words, Prefixes, and Suffixes

**Directions:** What is the root word in the following underlined words?

**Example:**

nicest

(A) nicer

(B) nice

(C) nices

(D) nicest

**Answer:**

(B) nice

---

8  bushes

(A) bush

(B) bushes

(C) bushe

(D) bus

---

9  busiest

(A) busie

(B) busy

(C) busies

(D) busi

---

10  knives

(A) nive

(B) kniv

(C) knive

(D) knife

---

11  dresses

(A) dress

(B) dresse

(C) dres

(D) dresses

---

12  baking

(A) bakin

(B) bake

(C) bak

(D) baki

---

**Directions:** Identify the **suffix** in each of the following underlined words.

**Example:**

allowing

(A) allow

(B) allowin

(C) ing

(D) all

**Answer:**

(C) ing

---

13  jumping

(A) jump

(B) ng

(C) ing

(D) jumping

---

14  helpless

(A) less

(B) le

(C) help

(D) les

---

**15** <u>leaving</u>

Ⓐ leave

Ⓑ ing

Ⓒ eing

Ⓓ ving

**16** What suffix do we add to the word <u>play</u> to mean "one who plays"?

Ⓐ er

Ⓑ or

Ⓒ ette

Ⓓ ed

**Directions:** Identify the **prefix** in each of the following underlined words.

**Example:**

<u>bicycle</u>

Ⓐ cycle

Ⓑ bicycle

Ⓒ bi

Ⓓ cle

**Answer:**

Ⓒ bi

**17** <u>displeased</u>

Ⓐ ed

Ⓑ di

Ⓒ dis

Ⓓ displease

**18** <u>export</u>

Ⓐ port

Ⓑ ex

Ⓒ exp

Ⓓ export

**19** <u>replayed</u>

Ⓐ play

Ⓑ ed

Ⓒ re

Ⓓ replay

**Directions:** Define the **prefix** in each of the following underlined words.

**20** What does the prefix <u>re</u> mean in the word <u>rebuild</u>?

Ⓐ to knock down

Ⓑ not to build

Ⓒ to build before

Ⓓ to build again

**21** What does the prefix <u>un</u> mean in the word <u>unstoppable</u>?

Ⓐ open

Ⓑ can't be stopped

Ⓒ stopped in the wrong place

Ⓓ sent away to be stopped

(See page 115 for answer key.)

## Compound Words

Compound words are created by combining two smaller words, such as *card* and *board* to become *cardboard*.

## What Third Graders Should Know

By third grade, most children know that many words in English have been combined to create new words. Your child should be able to come up with some compound words on her own and recognize others that she reads.

## What You and Your Child Can Do

**Compound Jumble.** Print a number of nouns on index cards. Have your child form as many compound words from these cards as possible.

**Compound Challenge.** Hang a long piece of paper from the refrigerator, and challenge your child to write down as many compound words as she can.

**Compounding Compounds.** Encourage your third grader to keep a notebook filled with favorite compound words. See how many she can accumulate.

**Crazy Compounds.** Using the index cards you made in the previous activity, have your child try to form deliberately silly compounds and make up crazy definitions for them.

**Compound Wordfind.** Give your child a magazine or newspaper and a highlighter. Set the stopwatch for two minutes, and have her highlight as many compound words as she can find.

**Sticky Note Scavenger Hunt.** Write down a list of compound words. Start with 10. Write the first part of the compound word on a sticky note, and tape it somewhere in the house with a blank sticky note beside it. Send your child off to find all 10 sticky notes. When your child finds one, have her finish the compound word. (For example, *sun*—could be *sunshine* or *sunbeam* or *suntan.*) Gather up the notes and read them together. For an extra challenge, try a backward compound hunt: Fill out the second half of a compound word, and ask your child to come up with the beginning. (So—*ball* might be *baseball* or *football* or *softball.*)

## What Tests May Ask

In third grade, standardized tests will include some questions about compound words. Usually the test asks students to choose the compound word from a group of choices.

## Practice Skill: Compound Words

**Directions:** Select the word that is made up of two words in the following choices.

**Example:**

Ⓐ baseball

Ⓑ scare

Ⓒ falcon

Ⓓ tighten

**Answer:**

Ⓐ baseball

---

22 Ⓐ sunshine

Ⓑ happiness

Ⓒ foolish

Ⓓ running

---

23 Ⓐ skied

Ⓑ skated

Ⓒ steamboat

Ⓓ filter

---

24 (A) houseboat

(B) jumping

(C) hiding

(D) beam

25 (A) wonderful

(B) window

(C) sunflower

(D) silliness

(See page 115 for answer key.)

## CHAPTER 7

# Capitalization and Punctuation

Capitalization and punctuation are a part of language mechanics that help students convey information to the reader. Third grade is the time to learn more detailed rules for punctuation and capitalization.

## What Third Graders Should Know

By third grade you have probably noticed your child is writing much more complete sentences and detailed stories. In third grade, students begin to learn more varied punctuation marks. They are also expanding their use of capital letters and using them correctly with some consistency.

The third-grade curriculum in most schools focuses on the use of capital letters in a wide variety of situations, including the first letter of sentences, proper names, initials within a name, the beginning of a sentence within a quote, and the salutation of a letter. By capitalizing and punctuating correctly, readers will be given a guideline to better understand your child's writing.

Punctuation is also an important skill taught thoroughly in third grade. Your child should be able to punctuate the end of a sentence using periods, question marks, and exclamation marks appropriately. He also should be familiar with quotation marks used to show that someone is talking. Third graders also focus on the correct use of commas in several situations: to set off items in a list, to set off a direct quote, to sepa-rate a dependent clause, and to separate the parts of dates. Other punctuation that is introduced this year includes apostrophes in contractions and in possessive nouns. However, apostrophes can still be difficult for some children in third grade. Correct punctuation in letter writing will also be introduced this year.

## What You and Your Child Can Do

The best way for children to learn proper capitalization and punctuation is to practice writing as often as possible. Don't be afraid to offer some gentle correction when your child makes a basic capitalization error. There are lots of ways you can get your child to practice.

**Write a Story.** Have your child write a story about a favorite hobby or experience, and go over it gently, pointing out glaring capitalization mistakes.

**Take a Letter!** Writing the addresses on envelopes is good practice for capitalization rules. Don't miss an opportunity to let your child help you address holiday cards and invitations. Encourage him to write a letter to a hero, political leader, sports figure, musician, or athlete. Make sure all the capital letters are correct in the address.

**Be the Editor for a Day.** Most third graders are passionate computer wizards. If you have a computer at home, write a paragraph or two for him, and make it as funny a story as you can. Include lots of capitalization errors, and then let your child edit the paragraph on the computer.

**Find a Pen Pal.** Ask your child to write a postcard to Aunt Sharon telling her about the fishing trip you just went on during vacation. Go over your child's first "sloppy copy" to check for punctuation mistakes, and then let him copy the words onto a postcard. Or have him write a postcard to his pet, and mail it to his home address. (This is a great way to keep track of vacations over the years; if you save these cards, after 20 years you'll have wonderful vacation memories, in addition to your child's writing practice!)

**Read Aloud.** One way to help remind your child to focus on punctuation is to have him read his work out loud. If your child seems to be having trouble with punctuation, get him to read to you a paragraph that he's written. When he does this, it's much more obvious to him where the sentence should end with a period or where a pause would indicate a comma. It just *sounds* right. Remind him that if he's not sure about punctuation, to read it to himself quietly to see if that helps steer him in the right direction.

**Keep a Diary.** Encourage your child to keep a diary. There are great-looking journals and diaries at stationery stores and bookstores, and they make nice gifts for children. Keeping a diary will allow your child a chance to get used to writing down his feelings and experiences. Don't worry yet about sophisticated colons, semicolons, dashes, quotation marks, and ellipses. For now, just have him concentrate on periods, question marks, and exclamation points—that's what the standardized tests will focus on as well.

**The Editor Is In.** This works just as well for punctuation as for capitalization; write a funny story on your computer, and put in lots of punctuation errors. Tell your child how many errors he should look for (it's less frustrating for children if you tell them how many mistakes there are).

## What Tests May Ask

Because standardized tests must be given in a format that will allow answer sheets to be scored by computer, the questions test a child's ability to *recognize* correct and incorrect punctuation when he sees it. Tests may present a choice of sentences and ask which one is punctuated correctly, or they may provide a sentence with several possibilities for punctuation and ask the child to choose where to place the period, comma, question mark, or exclamation mark.

## Practice Skill: Capitalization

**Directions:** Read these sentences. Choose the word that isn't capitalized but that should begin with a capital letter.

**Example:**

> For our vacation, we are going to philadelphia.
>
> (A) our
>
> (B) vacation
>
> (C) going
>
> (D) philadelphia

**Answer:**

> (D) philadelphia

---

**1** did you see the elephant at the zoo?

(A) you

(B) did

(C) elephant

(D) zoo

**2** I will address this letter to Frank j.
Baum.

   Ⓐ  I

   Ⓑ  address

   Ⓒ  Frank

   Ⓓ  j.

**3** Raising her head, she cried, "hey!
Look out!"

   Ⓐ  head

   Ⓑ  she

   Ⓒ  cried

   Ⓓ  hey

**4** dear John:

I would like to invite you to the
party.

   Ⓐ  dear

   Ⓑ  would

   Ⓒ  invite

   Ⓓ  you

**5** On the fifth of march, we went to the
theater.

   Ⓐ  fifth

   Ⓑ  march

   Ⓒ  went

   Ⓓ  theater

**Directions:** Choose the sentence that
shows correct capitalization.

**Example:**

   Ⓐ  Tom and Cindy are Going to
town today.

   Ⓑ  Are you going to make a
Pineapple cake?

   Ⓒ  On Tuesday, we will both go to
Paris.

   Ⓓ  where are you

**Answer:**

   Ⓒ  On Tuesday, we will both go to
Paris.

**6**  Ⓐ  In the Summer, Susan likes to
go swimming.

   Ⓑ  I don't like Molasses cookies.

   Ⓒ  Sam is going to move to
Southern georgia.

   Ⓓ  My favorite holiday comes in
October.

**7**  Ⓐ  Our little dog is a Golden
retriever.

   Ⓑ  Will you come to visit me in
Arizona?

   Ⓒ  At Midnight, the dog began to
howl.

   Ⓓ  We like to carve Pumpkins on
halloween.

**8** (A) "Look out!" she cried.

(B) Turning around, he said, "well, I think we should go."

(C) "are you going to bed yet?" She asked.

(D) I live at 314 Red School road.

---

**9** (A) Harry needs to write a thank you note to Uncle Sam.

(B) mom, can I go to the sleepover?

(C) don told his friend that he could not go.

(D) Debbie likes to sing tunes from *The sound of music.*

---

(See pages 115–116 for answer key.)

## Practice Skill: Punctuation

**Directions:** Choose the sentence that shows correct punctuation.

**Example:**

(A) Sarah, come right here?

(B) Look out!

(C) How old are you.

(D) Sarah ran down the hill

**Answer:**

(B) Look out!

---

**10** (A) I need carrots bread and milk.

(B) Let's take our books, tablets, and tape to school.

(C) Let's go for a swim", he said.

(D) What shall we do today.

---

**11** (A) After the movie, the boys went home.

(B) Today is October 15 2001.

(C) Yesterday was October, 14 2001.

(D) The car, is going too fast.

---

**12** (A) Where are you going.

(B) What kind, of dog is that.

(C) Sara, can you ride a bike!

(D) "I don't know," she said quietly.

---

**13** (A) Bill Larry and Sue are going to school together.

(B) Will you hurry up!

(C) Are you going to the fair.

(D) Jane please read the book.

---

(See page 116 for answer key.)

## CHAPTER 8

# Grammar Rules

By third grade, most children are fluent and capable readers and writers who know the appropriate grammar rules, including the regular and irregular uses of nouns, verbs, and adjectives, as well as the possessive forms of pronouns and the correct construction of sentences.

## What Third Graders Should Know

Most third graders have learned that our language has both regular and irregular forms, and they have learned to generalize the rules of the English language. They know what pronouns are and how to make them possessive, and they know that many verbs don't follow regular rules for the present and past tenses.

But language expression is more than a collection of nouns and verbs. By now, your child is able to understand the building blocks of written expression so she can judge when simple sentences are formed correctly.

Your child probably also knows how to form the plurals of most nouns simply by adding an *s: one horse, two horses.* At the same time, she should be aware that many nouns in our language don't follow this simple rule. There is *one goose* but *two geese, one army* but *two armies*—and *one deer* or *500 deer.* She also should understand possession with the addition of a simple apostrophe and an *s.* She is also beginning to learn irregularities, such as the fact that the possessive forms of nouns ending in an *s* sound simply require an apostrophe (*Dennis' hat*).

Your child will also have learned about pronouns, including masculine and feminine pronouns, plural pronouns, and neuter pronouns. She will continue to work on verbs and verb tenses, mastering the simple rules and also understanding the irregular verbs as well: *Today I go, yesterday I went, tomorrow I will go; today I bring, yesterday I brought.*

By third grade, she should understand what an adjective is and how to use the comparative forms by adding *-er* or *-est* to regular adjectives to describe something as being "more than" or the superlative "most." She should also be comfortable with the irregular adjectives: *If one piece of candy is* good, *two is* better.

## What You and Your Child Can Do

**Read!** While your child is in third grade, you should continue doing what you have been doing for some time to help teach her grammar—read! As you read from a wide variety of books in areas that interest you both, your child is exposed to the correct grammatical forms of English.

**Match Up Pictures to Actions.** Have your child cut out from magazines some pictures of things that can be described with nouns and paste them onto index cards. Then have her print different nouns, one each, on individual index cards. Have her match the appropriate noun with a picture.

**Play a Match Game.** Taking the cards you and your child made in the preceding activity, arrange matching sets (such as a picture of a baby crying and the word *cry*) face down in rows. The first player turns over two cards and tries to match the noun with the verb. Successful players get to keep the two matching cards and take another turn. An unsuccessful match is returned face down.

**Talk and Listen.** Reading isn't the only way to reinforce the language. In everyday conversation, you can reinforce proper grammar in subtle ways so that your child automatically learns the correct patterns of grammatical English. Learning proper grammar in the beginning is much easier than having to unlearn improper or sloppy uses of the language. Teachers may work very hard to develop English skills, but when it comes to proper usage of a child's native language, odds are the patterns she learns at home are most reinforcing. This is why it's so important for parents to model correct English usage for their children.

**Play Computer Games.** A host of computer games can help foster good grammatical skills through fun practice. *Kid Works Deluxe* (Davidson) encourages youngsters to create multimedia books, stories, poems, and more using words together with pictures and sounds. In *Grammar Games* (Davidson), kids can engage in four exciting rain forest activities as they solve problems of plurals and possessives, identify subject-verb agreements, edit sentences for proper verb usage, and recognize sentence fragments. The game includes a complete grammar guide that provides grammar rules and examples at the click of the mouse.

**Keep a Journal.** At this age, it can be helpful to give your child something to write *about*. What would life be like if you were 4 inches tall? If you could be any sort of animal, what would you be?

If you can get your child to enjoy writing, the extra practice in grammatical skills will really pay off. If your child is reluctant to write, let her use your computer. Write a question for her to explore ("What would life be like if you lived at the bottom of the ocean?"). Let her spend an extra 10 minutes at your computer typing an answer. If your child doesn't like to type (or isn't very fast), consider leaving her a "surprise" interview question on a tape recorder. Let her record her answer as she's curled up in bed. Whether she's writing or speaking, this will give her practice in good grammar skills.

**Invent Silly Stories.** Here's an activity that youngsters just seem to love. Buy some *Mad Libs* books—or make your own! Jot down a brief story, leaving blanks in crucial spots where words are left out. Without revealing what the story is about, ask the players to give you words that you'll use to fill in the story blanks. You'll ask for adjectives, nouns, verbs, or pronouns— sometimes a blank may require a plural form. As the players offer words, jot them down. Then read the story with the words in the blanks. For example, here's what a story of blanks might look like:

*One day the <u>NOUN</u> jumped into his <u>ADJEC-TIVE</u> convertible <u>NOUN</u> and drove off with his <u>ADJECTIVE</u> dog.*

Your child gives you the following words in response to the parts of speech that you've asked for:

1. rabbit
2. sharp
3. tree stump
4. crabby

The story would then be read:

*One day the <u>rabbit</u> jumped into his <u>sharp</u> convertible <u>tree stump</u> and drove off with his <u>crabby</u> dog.*

**Have Children Share Their Writing.** A fun activity, especially if your child has a friend over or you have several children near the same age, is to develop an ongoing story. This can be effective when accomplished on the computer, or it can be simply written by hand. Have one child start off a story and break off after a few sentences; then have the second child continue. Then the first child picks up the tale, and so on. Have the children pay special attention to parts of speech as they work on the story.

**Practice with Sentence Substitutes.** On a pad of Post-its, write the pronouns your child has learned (such as *I, me, hers, his*). Then on a blackboard or dry erase board, print a sentence in large letters, such as: *David went to the store.* Ask your child to read the sentence out loud, and then substitute a pronoun for *David.* The Post-it Note should be placed over the word *David* and then read again. Take turns making up sentences and attaching Post-it pronouns.

**Invent Sentence Stretchers.** Here's a good way to get your children thinking in creative ways when it comes to writing sentences. On 10 slips of paper write down 10 different verbs, one on each slip. Next write 10 nouns. Finally, take 4 slips of paper and write down each of these words: *when, where, why,* and *how.* The first player then draws a slip from the noun pile and one from the verb pile, together with one of the 4 *when-where-why-how* words. If a player draws the words *banana* and *glow* and a *when-where* word *why,* he would write: "The banana glows because he's happy."

**Write Poetry.** One of the best ways to broaden your child's use of adjectives is through poetry—reading poetry is effective, but having your child come up with her own is even better. Most children may need a bit of help, however. Try this writing exercise to jump-start the adjective flow:

_____, _____, _____ puppies,

_____, _____, _____ puppies,

Puppies, puppies, puppies.

Give your child a letter to start—let's say the letter *s.* Then she must come up with three adjectives beginning with *s* to describe the puppies—sweet, softy, sugarlump, an so on. Encourage creativity and watch what happens! You can create as many verses as you want and change to other subjects of interest to your child.

**Dear Author**... To get your child to practice writing skills, have her write a letter of appreciation to her favorite author or illustrator, explaining why she likes a particular book. Check over the grammar and usage, and make gentle corrections if necessary.

## What Tests May Ask

Third-grade teachers usually assess how well a child understands the right way to use parts of speech by grading written essays and by having children fill in blanks or provide short answers to questions. Most standardized tests today assess grammar skills by testing a child's ability to *recognize* correct usage. On such a test, a child must read a sentence and then choose the correct answer for the blank. Recognizing correct usage is much easier than trying to come up with the correct part of speech or usage on her own. While a few states are trying to initiate a writing sample as part of the test, most states in the country do not offer this type of test.

## Practice Skill: Parts of Speech

**Directions:** Read the following sentences and choose the correct noun to go in the blank.

**Example:**

Sarah lost her book. "Did you see _____ book?" her friend Tim asked their teacher.

Ⓐ Sarahs

Ⓑ Sarahes

Ⓒ Sarah

Ⓓ Sarah's

**Answer:**

Ⓓ Sarah's

1 There was one boy in the class. There were three ____ in the hall.

Ⓐ boyses

Ⓑ boy

Ⓒ boy's

Ⓓ boys

2 Sandy didn't believe in _____.

Ⓐ elfs

Ⓑ elves

Ⓒ elvs'

Ⓓ elve's

3 This ____ brim needs to be fixed.

Ⓐ hats

Ⓑ hat's

Ⓒ hats'

Ⓓ hatses

4 A herd of ____ raced through the broken fence.

Ⓐ cattle

Ⓑ cowes

Ⓒ cow

Ⓓ cattles

**Directions:** Read the sentence and choose the letter underneath the verb.

**Example:** He ate cake today.
    Ⓐ Ⓑ Ⓒ Ⓓ

Ⓐ He

Ⓑ ate

Ⓒ cake

Ⓓ today

**Answer:**

Ⓑ ate

5 Josh wondered how long the snow
    Ⓐ      Ⓑ      Ⓒ          Ⓓ
would last.

Ⓐ Josh

Ⓑ wondered

Ⓒ how

Ⓓ snow

**Directions:** Read the sentences below and choose the correct pronoun to go in the blank.

**Example:** George looked under his bed, but _____ could not find his puppy.

  Ⓐ he

  Ⓑ his

  Ⓒ him

  Ⓓ it

**Answer:**

  Ⓐ he

---

**6** If I don't find _____ scarf, I'll have to buy a new one.

  Ⓐ she      Ⓑ its

  Ⓒ her      Ⓓ hers

---

**7** Although he was tired, George did not sleep in _____ bed.

  Ⓐ he      Ⓑ she

  Ⓒ hers      Ⓓ his

---

**8** Cassie is a very good potter. _____ is a very good potter.

  Ⓐ She      Ⓑ Her

  Ⓒ He      Ⓓ Him

---

**9** Paige and Betsy love to dance. _____ love to dance.

  Ⓐ Hers      Ⓑ They

  Ⓒ Their      Ⓓ She

**10** Joe and Ben are going to play football. They will play with _____ ball.

  Ⓐ them      Ⓑ him

  Ⓒ yours      Ⓓ their

---

(See page 116 for answer key.)

## Practice Skill: Adjectives

**Directions:** Choose the sentence that is written correctly.

**Example:**

  Ⓐ My dog Sammie is pretty, but that dog is prettier, and Karen's dog is prettiest of all.

  Ⓑ It's cold than it was yesterday, but not as colder as it will be tomorrow.

  Ⓒ This game is hard than I thought it would be.

  Ⓓ This candy is good, but that one is gooder.

**Answer:**

  Ⓐ My dog Sammie is pretty, but that dog is prettier, and Karen's dog is prettiest of all.

**11**

   Ⓐ  Today I was tired, but yesterday I was even tireder.

   Ⓑ  Joe says this game is hard, but that game is harder.

   Ⓒ  This is a pretty dress, but that dress is even prettiest.

   Ⓓ  Yesterday it is hot, but two weeks ago it is even hotter.

**12**

   Ⓐ  This soup is delicious, but that soup is more better.

   Ⓑ  I think my dog is the best pet in the class.

   Ⓒ  John's cat is not as smarter as Sally's.

   Ⓓ  Justin is going to sang a pretty song.

(See page 116 for answer key.)

## CHAPTER 9

# Breaking It Down

The ability to read and fully understand the content involves a host of high-level verbal skills such as being able to identify the details of a story such as the main idea, where the story takes place, and the sequence of events. This type of analysis will enrich your child's understanding and enjoyment of literature.

Now that third graders are reading independently, they are more able to fully appreciate the fine points of literature, such as the development of the main idea and the construction of the plot. They will also more readily keep track of the sequence of events in nonfiction such as the historical account of how the American colonies defeated the British during the American Revolution. In later grades, their ability to analyze character and plot development will continue to mature.

## Main Idea and Details

The main idea may be clearly stated, or the reader may have to figure it out from the information given. Learning how to sum up the main idea of a paragraph, chapter, or story is a challenging but important task for third graders. At this age, typical third graders are really struggling to summarize their reading.

One way to help your child acquire this skill is to first focus on titles, which should sum up the entire story in a few words and predict what will be happening. The ability to provide a title for a story is important because it's closely related to the ability to understand the main idea.

## What Third Graders Should Know

Although second graders may find it challenging to sum up an entire story in just a few words, third graders are finding it becoming easier. By now, your third grader is developmentally mature enough to understand a passage's main idea. Third graders also should be able to come up with alternate titles for stories they read or watch on TV. The ability to provide a title for their stories requires relatively sophisticated reading comprehension skills that generally begin only at about late second grade and continue to develop in third grade.

## What You and Your Child Can Do

**Get Ready!** Before starting to read a book together, spend some time talking about the main idea of the book with your child. First check out the title: Ask him for his opinion about what the book might be about. Is *Little Men* a story about men? Then move on to the chapter titles. Ask your child if he can figure out what the chapter might be about by reading the title. What other titles might he come up with?

**Invent Title Alternates.** To boost your child's ability to summarize the main idea, brainstorm for "alternate titles" of story classics. Make them as funny as you want, but aim for a good summary of the story. Or choose a book without chapter titles, and have your child come up with his own.

**Write a Blurb.** One good way of getting to the main idea is to have your child come up with his own "cover blurb" that summarizes the story. To help him get started, let him read the back cover blurbs on a few of his favorite books. Then choose a book your child knows well, and see if he can come up with his own cover blurb by summarizing the main idea. Remind him that some back cover blurbs don't give complete summaries because the publisher is trying to entice the reader to read the book to find out more details.

## What Tests May Ask

Standardized tests for third graders will include some questions devoted to figuring out the main idea of a passage. Questions may ask a student to choose a main idea sentence, the best title, or a main topic that describes the passage.

Students also may be asked to choose supporting details that describe the main idea of a passage. When answering questions about the main idea, students should read the title and the passage very carefully in order to help decode the main idea.

## Practice Skill: Main Idea and Details

**Directions:** Read the following stories and then answer the questions that follow them.

### What Is a Galaxy?

Galaxies are huge regions of space containing billions of stars, planets, gas, dust, empty space, and perhaps a black hole. A spiral galaxy is a group of stars; the central group is surrounded by a halo and an invisible cloud of dark matter, with arms spiraling out like a pinwheel. The spiral shape is formed because the whole galaxy is spinning.

**Example:**

Galaxies are huge regions of

- (A) stars.
- (B) moons.
- (C) space.
- (D) universes.

**Answer:**

- (C) space.

---

1 What is this passage mostly about?
- (A) how fast the sun sets
- (B) what galaxies are
- (C) how ancient people measured time
- (D) what time the sun rises

---

2 Why are some galaxies called *spiral galaxies*?
- (A) They are cylindrical.
- (B) They are cone shaped.
- (C) They have arms like pinwheels.
- (D) They move in counterclockwise circles.

---

3 How did the galaxy become a spiral?
- (A) by the pull of black holes
- (B) by the pull of gravity
- (C) by the circling of the moon
- (D) by the spinning of the entire galaxy

**4** What would be another good title for this passage?

  (A) What Is a Spiral Galaxy?

  (B) Ancient Ways to Tell Time

  (C) Sun and Moon

  (D) For Every Season

## Making Honey

Bees make honey by first gathering a sweet liquid called *nectar* from flowers. The bees bring the nectar back to their hive in their stomachs. Inside the bees' stomachs is a chemical that helps turn the nectar into honey. When the bees get to the hive, they deposit the honey in an empty cell made of beeswax. As the nectar sits in the cell, the water in the nectar dries up and the chemicals that the bees added turn the substance into honey.

**5** What is the main idea of the passage?

  (A) how bees defend the hive

  (B) what bees like to eat

  (C) how bees make honey

  (D) how bees know where to find flowers

**6** How do the bees carry nectar back to the hive?

  (A) on their legs

  (B) on their backs

  (C) in their mouths

  (D) in their stomachs

**7** The passage says: "They deposit the honey in an empty cell." What does deposit mean in this sentence?

  (A) ate

  (B) drop off

  (C) fly

  (D) skim

**8** Which sentence is the best choice to come first in the paragraph below?

_____.

Box turtles can live more than 100 years. Some people say that turtles might be able to live for many hundreds of years if they did not have accidents. No one has been able to prove this, because turtles live longer than the people keeping records!

  (A) Certain types of land turtles weigh many hundreds of pounds.

  (B) Turtles live for a very long time.

  (C) Turtles have stumpy legs.

  (D) Turtles like to eat flies.

(See page 116 for answer key.)

## Sequence

The ability to understand the sequence in a piece of writing means you can figure out what comes first, next, and last in a story. It requires the ability to determine the main idea and supporting details and the ability to retell stories.

## What Third Graders Should Know

Most third graders have a solid understanding that events occur in a sequence, and they can differentiate easily between first, next, and last. In addition, they can explain a clustering of memorable events, problems, and solutions.

## What You and Your Child Can Do

**Play Title Scramble.** After you finish reading a favorite book, write down each chapter title on a slip of paper. Mix them up, and ask your child to see if he can put the titles back in correct order within one minute.

**Play Comic Strip Scramble.** Cut up a few weeks' worth of some comic strips. (You can laminate them if you wish.) Then mix them up, and have your child put them in correct sequence. What comes first? Next? Last?

**Make a Scrapbook.** Let your third grader make a scrapbook of his life, using old birthday cards, artwork, photos, old programs, and tickets. Let him add captions or narratives—chapter headings are even better! This will help him see the importance of *sequence* in telling a story—the story of his life.

**Make a List.** Have your child write in list form the directions for doing something familiar, such as making a peanut butter and jelly sandwich or making a bed.

## What Tests May Ask

Standardized tests that assess sequencing ability may ask students to figure out how sentences are related to each other, or they may ask questions about the sequence of events in the passage—perhaps what the main character did and in what order. To do well, students should remember to first scan the passage to get an idea of what the story is about before they answer the questions. In questions focusing on sequence, they should be alert for signal words such as *first, later, after, then, finally,* and *at last.*

## Practice Skill: Sequence

**Directions:** Read the passage. Choose the best answer to the following questions.

Joe needed to give his dog a bath. First he lined up the soap and the towels. Next, he filled the bathtub with warm water. Then he found Pal, his dog, and hooked the leash onto the dog. After 30 minutes, Joe was soaked, but Pal was clean! "Dad is going to be really surprised!" Joe told himself. His dad hadn't been sure Joe was responsible enough to have a dog. Now he would be proud!

**Example:**

Why did Joe fill the bathtub?

Ⓐ He wanted to take a bath.

Ⓑ He needed to clean the tub.

Ⓒ He needed to wash Pal.

Ⓓ He liked to play in the water.

**Answer:**

Ⓒ He needed to wash Pal.

---

9 What did Joe do first in the story?

Ⓐ filled the tub

Ⓑ lined up the soap and towels

Ⓒ put a leash on Pal

Ⓓ washed Pal

---

**10** Why did Joe want to wash Pal?

Ⓐ He liked to play with the dog.

Ⓑ Pal was dirty.

Ⓒ Joe was dirty.

Ⓓ Joe wanted to show his dad he could be responsible.

---

**11** The story uses the word <u>responsible</u>. What does the word <u>responsible</u> mean in this passage?

Ⓐ good with animals

Ⓑ smart and funny

Ⓒ capable and mature

Ⓓ popular

---

(See page 116 for answer key.)

## Characters and Settings

A good book is rich in details about the characters and the environment in which they live. Characters and settings are two of the important elements of literature. Caring about a character makes us care about the story itself, and being able to empathize with characters and understand their motivation is central to enjoying what we read. Likewise, an interesting or compelling setting adds immeasurably to our enjoyment of what we read.

## What Third Graders Should Know

By third grade, most children begin to note details about their favorite stories, such as the setting and the time in which the story takes place. They should be able to understand more complex details about characters as well, such as the relationships among the characters and their motives and moods. They can appreciate details about a character's height, build, likes, dislikes, and actions if the writer discusses them and they have a bearing on the story.

By third grade, your child should understand that characters are more than cardboard cutouts—they have flaws and good points. Bad characters aren't all bad, and good characters aren't perfect. Just as he begins to see people around him in an increasingly complex way, he is also gradually extending those skills to the people he meets in books.

For example, your child may read a book about Harry Potter and understand that although he sometimes broke the rules, he was not a bad guy and could even be considered a hero.

## What You and Your Child Can Do

**Make a Stage Set.** As you read a story with your child, especially if it has a strong setting, get out a big sheet of white paper at the end of the story and explore the structure you just read about. If your child just finished *Harry Potter,* have him draw the Hogwarts' castle. Put in all the rooms, staircases, towers, kitchens, and so on. Add rugs, pictures, and furnishings.

**Play Who's Who.** After you finish reading a story with your child, or after your child finishes a book, have him draw a picture of his favorite character. Use the clues found in the book: What does the character look like? Wear?

**Make a Diorama.** It's important to have your third grader pay attention to the descriptions of the settings that appear in the books he reads. Choose a book to read together and pay special attention to the clues the author gives about setting—place, time of year, and location. Get a cardboard box and create that setting to make it look as much like the setting in the book as possible. Use paints, markers, material, glue, buttons, glitter—anything you can think of to make the diorama come alive.

## What Tests May Ask

Standardized tests for this age will assess your child's understanding of a character by presenting a passage and then asking him to answer questions about the character and the character's motivation.

Your child should read the passage closely, looking for clues about how the character feels and what the person is like. Likewise, questions about setting that appear in given passages can help determine if your child is paying attention to these important written clues.

## Practice Skill: Characters and Settings

**Directions:** Read the passage. Choose the best answer to each question.

### The New Girl

Emily walked slowly into the crowded classroom. Kids were sitting at their desks laughing and talking to each other. No one looked at her, and her backpack felt heavy in her hands as she walked into the room.

How she missed Fiona and Emma from her old school! They would always have something funny to tell her first thing in the morning.

"Emily!" she heard someone call. "Hey, Emily!" She turned and saw a red-haired girl smiling from her desk in the corner. "Come on over and sit with me!" the girl called, motioning to her.

**Example:**

Why is Emily nervous?

Ⓐ  She's worried about a test.

Ⓑ  She is new at school.

Ⓒ  She's performing in a play.

Ⓓ  She forgot her books.

**Answer:**

Ⓑ  She is new at school.

12  How does Emily feel?

Ⓐ  excited about being in a new school

Ⓑ  angry about leaving the old school

Ⓒ  tired from carrying her books

Ⓓ  anxious about being the new girl

13  Where does this story take place?

Ⓐ  in the auditorium

Ⓑ  in a classroom

Ⓒ  in the cafeteria

Ⓓ  in the gym

14  What is the location of this story like?

Ⓐ  silent and empty

Ⓑ  noisy and crowded

Ⓒ  dark and scary

Ⓓ  bright and hot

15  How does Emily probably feel when the red-haired girl calls her name?

Ⓐ  angry

Ⓑ  relieved

Ⓒ  lonesome

Ⓓ  mad

(See page 116 for answer key.)

## CHAPTER 10

# Reading Comprehension

Reading comprehension—that is, understanding what has been read—is of great importance in third grade, as students become more adept at understanding stories in general. No longer do children this age have to struggle along, pausing to puzzle out every few words they encounter. Reading comprehension is considered to be a higher-order mental process that involves putting together a whole series of skills, including summarizing, predicting, sequencing, and drawing conclusions.

## What Third Graders Should Know

While second graders begin to critically evaluate what they read, by third grade students are much more comfortable in reading and understanding on many levels. Third graders can understand cause and effect, and predict and draw conclusions based on the information they have read. They can pick out the implied feelings and motivations of characters they read about, which allows them to compare and contrast one story or idea with another.

## What You and Your Child Can Do

**Read.** It's not too late to start if you've been neglecting reading to your child, and you should continue to do so if you have been reading out loud to her for some time. Reading out loud helps your child get used to following the thread of a story and understanding the events as she hears them. Continue reading to her and let her read to you.

**Read Magazines.** Subscribe or buy age-appropriate magazines such as *Stone Soup, American Girl,* or *National Geographic Junior.*

**Just the Facts, Ma'am.** Encourage your child to read a variety of newspapers, and give her the "who what when where and why" quiz. Point out short articles in the newspaper or your magazines that you think would interest her. If she has trouble reading the articles, help her. After she's finished, get a notebook and ask her the "who what where when and why" of the article. See how many she can name!

**View a Story from "Other Eyes."** This activity is a good way to get your child to think about how the story might change if it were told from another perspective. This activity works very well for tales with a strong moral. After you finish reading the story with your child, ask her how the story might be different if it were told from a different perspective.

**Help Your Child.** You can boost your child's comprehension by encouraging her to make predictions as she reads, compare and contrast stories, and think about characters and settings. Help your child talk about causes and effects, help her infer meaning, and expand her vocabulary.

**Jump Ahead.** If your child reads ahead in the book you're reading to her at night, don't scold! Just ask her to summarize the chapters you've missed, and keep going.

## Predicting Outcomes

Being able to predict the outcome of a story will help improve a child's reading comprehension. To be a good reader, she will have to become a good guesser—what might the character do next, what might happen in the next paragraph, how might the story end?

## What Third Graders Should Know

Third graders are getting better at predicting outcomes as they become more confident readers and risk takers. By this age they have learned enough about the world to be ready to make some intelligent guesses about how the story will turn out.

## What You and Your Child Can Do

**Predict!** Get your child into the habit of predicting events by asking her to predict everyday events—not just things in books. When you go out to eat, ask her to predict what Dad is going to order. What might Aunt Louise give her for her birthday? While you're waiting in the doctor's office, ask her to predict what the man across the room does for a living. Are there any clues in clothes or attitude?

**Practice.** You can help your child learn to take risks by doing lots of predicting. When you choose a book together, ask: Are you going to like this book? As you begin to read, ask her what she thinks the book is about. What does she think might happen next?

**Play Magazine ESP.** When you're in a bookstore, stop by the magazine section with your child. Look at the titles and ask her what she thinks the stories might be about.

## What Tests May Ask

Standardized tests for third graders will assess their ability to predict the outcome by presenting a passage and asking: What do you think will happen next? What do you think will happen in the end? Tests also may present a title and ask third graders to predict what the story might be about.

## Practice Skill: Predicting Outcomes

**Directions:** Read the passage. Choose the best answer for each question.

**Example:**

What is the best title for this passage?

Martin Luther King, Jr., was a great leader in the struggle for equal rights for African-Americans. He believed the government should treat people equally, no matter what their color or religion. He thought that people should live in peace.

(A) The Beliefs of Martin Luther King, Jr.

(B) Famous Holidays

(C) Why We Wear Green on St. Patrick's Day

(D) Living in Peace

**Answer:**

(A) The Beliefs of Martin Luther King, Jr.

### Story

The Eiffel Tower is one of the great landmarks of Paris. Built for the Paris World's Fair in 1889, it looks like a giant skeleton rising up over the French city. But when it was first built, many Parisians hated it! The tower is almost 1,000 feet tall and has a restaurant at the top.

**1** What is the best title for this passage?

- Ⓐ The Monuments of France
- Ⓑ The Eiffel Tower: A French Sensation
- Ⓒ I Like France
- Ⓓ Great Restaurants in France

**Directions:** Read the following questions and choose the correct answers.

**2** What is a book titled *Midnight Walks, Spooky Scary Stories* most likely to be about?

- Ⓐ a tall tale about kittens and their adventures
- Ⓑ a mystery involving secrets in a clock
- Ⓒ a collection of frightening tales
- Ⓓ a sad story about a family who loses everything in a fire

**3** The best title for a book about the life of a boy named Huck Finn is probably

- Ⓐ *The Adventures of Huck Finn.*
- Ⓑ *A Tale of Rabbits.*
- Ⓒ *Wynken, Blynken, and Nod.*
- Ⓓ *The Encyclopedia of Sea Creatures.*

**Directions:** Read the following passage and then choose the most logical sentence that describes what would happen next.

Sarah straightened her hat and riding jacket. Carefully she brushed some dust off her pony's legs. After lengthening her stirrups, she climbed up on a rock and mounted. Adjusting her hat brim, she gathered the reins.

**4** Ⓐ With a deep breath, she cantered into the horse show ring.

- Ⓑ The pony ate some hay in his stall.
- Ⓒ The sun went behind a cloud.
- Ⓓ Sarah unsaddled the pony and walked away.

**Directions:** Read the following passage. Choose the statement that best describes what the story will probably be about.

It was a dark and stormy night. The trees crashed against the old house and a shutter creaked mournfully on its squeaky hinges.

**5** Ⓐ The story will probably be a scary mystery.

- Ⓑ The story will probably be very funny.
- Ⓒ The story will probably be about happy farm animals.
- Ⓓ The story will probably be about science facts.

Pizza is found all over Italy. Each part of the country has its own special kind.

6  Ⓐ  This story will probably be a biography.

   Ⓑ  This story will probably be a factual article about pizza.

   Ⓒ  This story will probably make people laugh.

   Ⓓ  This story will probably be about a happy family in Rome.

(See page 116 for answer key.)

## Drawing Conclusions

A conclusion is a sort of judgment that a person makes by taking various clues into consideration. If your child walks into her friend's house and she sees all her friends there and they're wearing pajamas, she can conclude that there's a slumber party going on. In reading, your child will be expected to gather the clues planted by the author and make conclusions as a result of those clues.

## What Third Graders Should Know

By third grade your child should be able to appreciate the deeper meanings and subtle messages embedded in many stories and understand the characters' motivations. This means she has developed not only the ability to understand the words presented but also to draw inferences from sometimes-subtle wording and implied action.

## What You and Your Child Can Do

You can help your child learn how to reach conclusions and make inferences by gently guiding her to gather clues and then sum up what she's learned. For example, let's say your child reads a book about Canada geese in which she learns

that a male and female stay together for life, raising the babies together. You can then ask her what conclusions she can make about mother and father Canada geese. You're looking for an answer along these lines: They are loving parents who take good care of their babies.

**Ask Questions.** As you finish a story with your child, ask her questions that require her to read between the lines. The author may not come right out and describe everything in a chapter, but your child should be able to figure out subtle clues through inferences.

**Play Conclusion Caper.** Here's a good game for a wet weekend when your child has nothing to do. Get a set of index cards and write a series of numbered clues, one to a card. Hide them around the house for your child to find. Once she finds them all (tell her how many you've hidden so it's not too hard), have her read the clues in order and then come to a conclusion. Here are some sample clues:

1. At the store I got my grocery cart.
2. I bought gingerbread mix, flour, icing, sprinkles, peppermint sticks, and chocolate wafers.
3. I went to the dairy case.
4. I got butter, milk, and eggs.
5. I went to the department store.
6. I bought a set of special molds.
7. I went back home.
8. We're going to have lots of fun today in the kitchen!

   **Conclusion:** We're making a gingerbread house!

## What Tests May Ask

Standardized tests will assess how well your child can make conclusions and draw inferences from written material by presenting a story and asking questions about that passage.

Your child should read the entire passage first, looking for clues to help answer the questions. Once she draws a conclusion about what she's read, she should look for at least two details in the passage to support the answer.

## Practice Skill: Drawing Conclusions

**Directions:** Read the passage. Choose the best answer to each question.

### The Goat

Becca and Cassie were pushing their bikes along a country road. The sun was beating down, and the girls' clothes were damp. "Look!" Becca cried, pointing to a pasture full of goats. A very little goat kid was outside the fence, it's tiny foot tangled in the wire. Its anxious mother was on the other side, bleating loudly.

Cassie bent down and inspected the fence. There was a small place in the dirt beneath the fence where little hoof prints were clearly visible.

"Oh, the poor little guy!" Becca said. "I'll help you," she cried, reaching out toward the kid.

**Example:**

You can tell from the story that the weather is

Ⓐ   rainy.

Ⓑ   hot and humid.

Ⓒ   icy cold.

Ⓓ   snowing.

**Answer:**

Ⓑ   hot and humid.

**7**   What will probably happen next?

Ⓐ   A snake will bite Cassie.

Ⓑ   Becca will rescue the kid.

Ⓒ   Cassie will rescue the kid.

Ⓓ   The girls will walk away and leave the kid trapped.

**8**   Who is Cassie?

Ⓐ   Becca's aunt

Ⓑ   Becca's mother

Ⓒ   the goat

Ⓓ   Becca's friend

**Directions:** Read the passage and answer the question.

The teacher sent Sandy to the office for throwing a pencil at Tara. As Sandy left the room, he protested: "I didn't do it!" Jo grinned as she saw Sandy leave the class and thought to herself, "I got away with it." Who hit Tara with a pencil?

**9**   Ⓐ   Sandy

Ⓑ   Tara

Ⓒ   Jo

Ⓓ   the teacher

(See page 116 for answer key.)

### Cause and Effect

*Cause and effect* simply means something happens that leads to something else. In *Heidi,* the main character goes to live with her crusty grandfather, who becomes a caring person again. The cause: Heidi goes to live with her grandfather. The effect: He becomes a caring person again.

## What Third Graders Should Know

Third graders know very well that for every cause there is an effect. If they don't brush their teeth, they will get cavities. If they don't do their homework, their teacher will be displeased. They have learned that stories can be relied upon to have causes and effects too. Something happens in a story and something else occurs as a result.

## What You and Your Child Can Do

**Play Rube Goldberg.** Explain to your child who Rube Goldberg was, and then sit down with her to design her own machine. Decide what you'd like to accomplish (pour orange juice in the morning, for example), and then start off with a drawing of one piece of the machine to do that.

**Make a Game.** This is a terrific activity your third grader will love that also helps teach the idea of cause and effect. To make your own game board, take an old game board and cover it with wrapping paper, design side down. (Most wrapping paper is plain white on the inside.) If your child's favorite book is *The Wind in the Willows*, draw Toad's house at the top corner of the board, and Mole's hole at the bottom opposite corner. Now connect the two with a winding path of circles. In every other circle, write things like "Toad gets a car. Go ahead two" or "Meets a stoat. Go back two." As you play the game, read the messages out loud. Explain which is the cause and which is the effect: "Oh, look. I met a weasel. I must go back two." First player to reach Toad's mansion wins.

**Play "Before That!"** Take opportunities in everyday life to point out cause and effect by asking your child to imagine what happened just before. If you see a cat racing across the street, ask your child to imagine what happened right before this to set the cat off. If you see a man fixing a flat tire by the side of the road, ask your child what might have happened right before this to trigger the event.

**Make Silly Science.** Science is all about cause and effect. Buy a "slime science" or other silly science kit for you and your child to play with. Or try your own experiments around the house. Try making a baking powder volcano: Have your child shape clay into a volcano shape, with a crater at the top. Drop in some baking powder (add food coloring if you want) and then drizzle on vinegar. Watch the lava flow!

## What Tests May Ask

Standardized tests for the third grade usually assess cause and effect by presenting a passage and then asking questions about the passage. To answer the questions, the reader must understand what is going on in the story and to be able to infer what caused something to happen. Students should look for clue words such as *because, so, since,* or *as a result* that indicate cause and effect.

## Practice Skill: Cause and Effect

**Directions:** Read this passage and then answer the question.

Jane seemed very unhappy in her new school. She spoke only Spanish at home and often didn't understand the teacher. She didn't do well in tests and the other kids teased her, calling her "stupid."

**Example:**

Why did the kids tease Jane?

Ⓐ  because she was mean

Ⓑ  because Jane seemed slow

Ⓒ  because Jane was a brat

Ⓓ  because she didn't understand the teacher

**Answer:**

    Ⓑ  because Jane seemed slow

---

**10**  Why did Jane have trouble in class?

    Ⓐ  She was dumb.

    Ⓑ  She was bad.

    Ⓒ  She didn't understand the language.

    Ⓓ  She spoke French.

---

## CHAPTER 11

# Literary Genres

Many types of literature are introduced in third grade, including poetry, biography, tall tales, fantasy, fact, and fiction. Very young readers accept what they read literally—if it's written down, it must be true—but by third grade readers have become far more sophisticated and harder to fool. They know that animals don't talk and that science fiction is just that—fiction. By this age, your child is beginning to discern reality from fantasy in what he sees on television, in the stories you read to him, and in what he reads.

By third grade, children understand the difference between fact and opinion. They can discuss and give examples of all genres of literature, and they can reproduce them in their own writing. They can see a major idea or theme in a piece of writing, and they can collect evidence of that theme.

## Facts versus Opinions

*Facts* are simply bits of information that are true: Whales are mammals, and dogs are canines. An *opinion* is a statement of what someone thinks or believes: "I think Ronald Reagan was a good president" or "*XYZ* is the best brand of orange juice."

## What Third Graders Should Know

There is a big difference between a fact and an opinion, and by third grade your child will begin to understand this difference quite clearly.

While earlier readers may accept anything they read as the literal truth, third grade children are becoming much more able to discern the difference between a factual piece of writing and a biased or personal opinion.

## What You and Your Child Can Do

**Fact or Fiction?** Help your third grader tell the difference between the two. Read a letter to the editor and news story on the same subject—out loud. Discuss which contained facts and which contained opinions.

**Fact-Opinion Survey.** Using a sheet of paper and a newspaper, tell your child you're having a "fact-opinion hunt." Divide the plain paper into two columns, one labeled "facts" and one labeled "opinions." Open the newspaper to the advertisement section, and have your child write down "facts" or "opinions" under the appropriate column. Set a time limit of two or three minutes. If there is more than one player, stage a competition. Once the bell rings, discuss the facts and opinions and the difference between them.

**Fun Ads.** Have your child write an ad (and illustrate it) for a fictional product. Let him be as outrageous as he wants. Discuss how an advertisement may contain opinions, not just the facts.

**Critic for a Day.** To help your child see the difference between fact and opinion, appoint him "family critic." Have him vote thumbs up or down on various TV shows, video games, or movies for the family. Have him describe the show (the facts) and then give a rating (his opinion). Point out the difference.

## What Tests May Ask

Standardized tests for third grade will assess whether your child can tell the difference between fact and opinion. Your child will be expected to read a passage and then answer questions about whether each idea in the passage is a fact or opinion. To decide which is which, your child should look for something that can be proven true—that's a fact. Something that is a feeling or a belief is an opinion.

## Practice Skill: Facts versus Opinions

**Directions:** Read the passage. Choose the best answer to each question.

### Story

John Brown is up for election for a position on the school board. John grew up in this county. He is married with two children. He works very hard. John has lots of friends in the community. He's an honest man and will work hard for everyone. So get out there and vote for John Brown—he's the best!

**Example:**

What is the article about?

- Ⓐ the school board
- Ⓑ John Brown's family
- Ⓒ John Brown's desire to run for the school board
- Ⓓ community spirit

**Answer:**

- Ⓒ John Brown's desire to run for the school board

1 Which idea from the passage is a fact?

- Ⓐ John Brown is the best.
- Ⓑ John Brown works hard.
- Ⓒ John Brown is an honest man.
- Ⓓ John Brown is running for a job on the school board.

2 Which idea from this passage is an opinion?

- Ⓐ John Brown is running for a job on the school board.
- Ⓑ John Brown was born in this county.
- Ⓒ John Brown is the best.
- Ⓓ John Brown is married.

3 The author's purpose in this passage is to

- Ⓐ discuss the school board.
- Ⓑ convince you to vote for John Brown.
- Ⓒ help you learn about government.
- Ⓓ get you to vote for president.

(See page 116 for answer key.)

## Reality versus Fantasy

What is real and what is fantasy? The difference between what is real and what is only imagined is an important one in literature, and in third grade students are introduced to both genres.

## What Third Graders Should Know

Third graders are usually introduced to a wide range of classic fantasy stories, and they are taught to compare these rich forms of literature with reality-based stories.

## What You and Your Child Can Do

**Reality Check.** As you read a child's fantasy book (such as Madeleine L'Engle's *A Wind in the Door*), discuss with your child the difference between reality and fantasy. Get a notebook and on one side of the page, write "reality" and on the other, "fantasy." After reading a chapter in *Wind,* take turns writing sentences about what could really happen under "reality" and what couldn't happen under "fantasy":

| Reality | Fantasy |
|---|---|
| Meg is worried about her brother. | There is such a thing as a cherubim. |
| Charles Wallace makes hot cocoa. | Meg travels into Charles' mitochondrion. |

## What Tests May Ask

Standardized tests in third grade usually assess a child's understanding of the difference between reality and fantasy by presenting a passage and asking the child to discern which statements are true and which are grounded in fantasy.

## Practice Skill: Reality versus Fantasy

**Directions:** Choose the correct answer for the following questions.

4 Which of these sentences is true?

   (A) Dogs can do tricks.

   (B) Humans have walked on Mars.

   (C) Cats can speak.

   (D) There are such things as dragons.

---

5 Which of these sentences is based on fantasy?

   (A) Humans have 10 toes.

   (B) Geese can lay golden eggs.

   (C) You can write on paper.

   (D) Airplanes fly in the air.

---

(See page 116 for answer key.)

## Biography

In most third-grade classrooms, a certain amount of time is spent reading and discussing biographies of leaders in sports, science, medicine, government, and history. No matter what interests your child may have, it should be possible to find a biography that he will enjoy reading.

## What Third Graders Should Know

Most third graders have a solid understanding of what a biography is—a story about a person—and what kinds of information would be expected to be included in a biography. He should have read in class several biographies of different types of people from different times in history.

## What You and Your Child Can Do

**Relative Bio.** Here's a great project to cement family relationships. At the next family gathering, let your child take a tape recorder and interview family members. Have your child write down a series of questions and record the answers. Then let him choose one family member to write a "biography" about. Gather photos of that person, and have your child illustrate the photos with a story of that person's life. (This can make a good gift when it's completed, too!)

**Tonight Show.** After you read a biography with your child, have him take "the mike" and sit down for an interview. Have your child pretend he is the character in the book you've just read, and ask him all kinds of questions. See how well he can put himself into the character's shoes.

**Your Child's Biography.** What better way to learn all about biography than to write his own? Get your child some sheets of paper, colored pens, photographs, and stickers, and have him write his own biography. Make sure he includes all of the most important points that have occurred so far in his life. (Making a brief outline of his life might help him organize his thoughts.) Include a construction paper cover and staple the sheets together.

**Mini Bio.** After your child finishes reading a favorite book, have him write a biography of one of the characters in the book. For example, if he loves the *Goosebumps* series, have him write a biography about a minor character in the series.

## What Tests May Ask

In assessing students' understanding of biographical writing, standardized tests during the third grade will present a brief biographical sketch and then ask children a series of questions about the passage. These questions may ask children to determine the genre, or they may ask specific questions about one aspect of the passage.

## Practice Skill: Biography

**Directions:** Read the following passages and choose the correct answers to the questions that follow each passage.

Walt Disney was born in Chicago on December 5, 1901. Walt was raised on a farm in Missouri. He sold his first sketches to neighbors when he was only seven. When he grew up, he worked as a cartoonist. He is best known for creating Mickey Mouse and building Disneyland and Walt Disney World.

**6** Walt Disney was

 Ⓐ   the first artist in space.

 Ⓑ   the creator of Mickey Mouse.

 Ⓒ   the first teacher to go to Disneyworld.

 Ⓓ   the first farmer to build a roller coaster.

**7** Disney was raised

 Ⓐ   in the city.

 Ⓑ   in Disneyworld.

 Ⓒ   in a circus.

 Ⓓ   on a farm.

Wilbur and Orville Wright made the first flight in a real airplane. They flew their plane called *The Flyer* at Kitty Hawk, North Carolina, on December 17, 1903. The plane flew 120 feet in 12 seconds. Their next flight went 852 feet, and the plane was airborne for almost a minute.

**8** The Wrights are remembered as

(A) inventors of the steam engine.

(B) inventors of the gas engine.

(C) inventors of the first successful airplane.

(D) inventors of electricity.

**9** The first successful airplane ride occurred in

(A) West Virginia.

(B) North Carolina.

(C) North Dakota.

(D) Maine.

(See page 116 for answer key.)

## Poetry

Poetry is a popular genre in third grade, and the language of poets is a wonderful way to stretch a child's imagination and love of language. In third grade, your child should understand what makes a poem, the rhythmic effects of certain sounds and repetitions, and how words can be used to help form mental pictures.

Popular poetry books for children this age include *A Child's Garden of Verses* (Robert Louis Stevenson), *Roald Dahl's Revolting Rhymes* (Roald Dahl), and *When Whales Exhale and Other Poems by Young People* (Constance Levy).

## What Third Graders Should Know

Poignant metaphors and powerful imagery come easily to children, who often develop real confidence in their writing ability at this age. Because a poem can be short—and doesn't always have to conform to traditional rules—it often appeals even to reluctant writers.

## What You and Your Child Can Do

**Read Aloud.** Poems often sound best when read aloud. Read often to your third grader, who will appreciate the wit of poets such as Ogden Nash or Shel Silverstein. After you read a poem, ask your child what he likes about the poem and what the poem makes him feel or think about. Ask your child how the poet uses sound to make the poem more effective. Remember, the best way to help your child become a better poet is to read poetry.

**Read Poetry on a Stage.** Put on a poetry reading at your house. Turn the lights down low, light lots of candles, and let your child choose some good background music. Then let him read a few chosen poems. Or have your child make up a dance routine to go with a favorite poem.

**Have a Poetry Party.** Get several different books of poetry, and read a few poems from each book out loud. Talk about how the poems are different and why the poet may have chosen to write in a particular style.

**It Doesn't Have to Rhyme.** Children this age assume all poetry must rhyme. Get a book or two of poems that don't rhyme. You can always count on e.e. cummings, but if his poetry seems too adult for your child, choose a book such as *Light and Shadow* by Myra Cohn Livingston, which is a book of free verse that appeals to this age group.

**Have a Poetry Contest.** Urge your child to enter poetry contests—they are fun, and he could win a prize! There are plenty of literary magazines that accept children's poetry such as *Stone Soup* or *Highlights for Children*. Check out online poetry contests, such as this site: The Number 1 Poetry Site for Kids on the Web, http://www.gigglepoetry.com/contests.html.

## What Tests May Ask

Standardized tests in third grade assess a child's understanding of poetry by presenting a poem or part of a poem, and then asking specific questions about the poem. Questions may ask about the poet's intentions, specific topics within the poem, the title, and purpose of the poem.

## Practice Skill: Poetry

**Directions:** Read the poem and answer the questions that follow each poem.

### The Land of Counterpane
By Robert Louis Stevenson

When I was sick and lay a-bed,
I had two pillows at my head,
And all my toys beside me lay,
To keep me happy all the day.

And sometimes for an hour or so
I watched my leaden soldiers go,
With different uniforms and drills,
Among the bed-clothes, through the hills;

And sometimes sent my ships in fleets
All up and down among the sheets;
Or brought my trees and houses out,
And planted cities all about.

I was the giant great and still
That sits upon the pillow-hill,
And sees before him, dale and plain,
The pleasant land of counterpane.

**10**  What does the author mean by the word "bed-clothes"?

   Ⓐ  shirts

   Ⓑ  blankets and sheets

   Ⓒ  bathrobes and slippers

   Ⓓ  toothbrushes

**11**  From this poem, you can tell

   Ⓐ  how many toys the poet had when he was a child.

   Ⓑ  what the poet did when he was sick.

   Ⓒ  that the poet doesn't like to sleep.

   Ⓓ  it's Christmas time.

**12**  What does the poet mean when he says, "I was the giant great and still"?

   Ⓐ  He was a very tall child.

   Ⓑ  He was a very slow child.

   Ⓒ  He was pretending to be a giant looking over his land.

   Ⓓ  He was asleep.

### Twinkle, Twinkle Little Star
By Jane Taylor

Twinkle, twinkle, little star,
How I wonder what you are.
Up above the world so high,
Like a diamond in the sky.

When the blazing sun is gone,
When he nothing shines upon,
Then you show your little light,
Twinkle, twinkle, all the night.
Then the trav'ller in the dark,
Thanks you for your tiny spark,
He could not see which way to go,
If you did not twinkle so.

In the dark blue sky you keep,
And often thro' my curtains peep,
For you never shut your eye,
Till the sun is in the sky.

'Tis your bright and tiny spark,
Lights the trav'ller in the dark:
Tho' I know not what you are,
Twinkle, twinkle, little star.

13  What does the author mean that the star "never shuts his eye"?

Ⓐ  The sun never sets.

Ⓑ  The stars never stop twinkling.

Ⓒ  The moon never goes down.

Ⓓ  The stars never fall out of the sky.

14  What does the author compare a star to in the poem?

Ⓐ  the sun

Ⓑ  an icicle

Ⓒ  a rose

Ⓓ  a diamond

(See page 116 for answer key.)

## CHAPTER 12

# Study Skills

During third grade, students spend time learning to improve their basic study skills, such as finding different types of information and using basic resources and reference works. These resources include encyclopedias, dictionaries, and atlases. Many children begin to use the newspaper to learn about current events.

In order to use these various resources, students need to be comfortable with alphabetizing words, using the guide words on a reference book page, and understanding dictionary entries. They also need to know what kinds of information they may find in different parts of a book.

Study skills are vital to students for their entire school career, so you can expect your child's teacher to continue discussing basic study skills during this year.

## Alphabetizing

Words are alphabetized according to their first letter:

about

because

myself

If all the first letters are the same, alphabetizing moves to the second letter:

about

across

again

If the first and second letters are the same, alphabetizing moves to the third letter:

does

done

door

## What Third Graders Should Know

By third grade, your child should feel comfortable with alphabetizing, although putting words in alphabetical order to the third letter may still be an effort for some children. By the end of the year, however, third graders are expected to be able to alphabetize words to the third letter.

## What You and Your Child Can Do

**Alphabet in the Middle.** For this game, give your child two words. Have her come up with a word that would fit in between the two. Start out with words that begin with different letters. As she gets better, use words with the same first letters. Finally, move on to words with the same first two letters.

**List of Words.** Give your child three lists of words—one set with different first letters, another set with the same first letters, and a third set with the same first two letters. Have her alphabetize them for a preset time. See how long each list takes. If she enjoys this activity, work on improving her "personal best" time.

**Personal Library.** Setting up a corner of your child's room as an alphabetized personal library is one way of showing how important you think books are. Once you've gotten the shelves together, let her set up the books herself. This will provide a good bit of practice in alphabetization.

## What Tests May Ask

Standardized tests in third grade will ask your child a series of questions about alphabetizing, assessing her skill to the third letter. Typically, the tests will present a list of words and ask your child to choose the word that will come next—or to choose the one word that does not fit.

## Practice Skill: Alphabetizing

**Directions:** In the following list of alphabetical words, choose the word that comes next in correct alphabetical order from the choices below.

**Example:**

> country    dirt    friend
>
> Ⓐ    always
>
> Ⓑ    been
>
> Ⓒ    cane
>
> Ⓓ    guess

**Answer:**

> Ⓓ    guess

---

**1**    anyone    excited    school

> Ⓐ    beginning
>
> Ⓑ    women
>
> Ⓒ    right
>
> Ⓓ    meant

---

**2**    been    before    beginning

> Ⓐ    bear
>
> Ⓑ    ban
>
> Ⓒ    believe
>
> Ⓓ    be

---

**3**    wear    Wednesday    were

> Ⓐ    west
>
> Ⓑ    wasn't
>
> Ⓒ    weave
>
> Ⓓ    well

---

(See page 116 for answer key.)

## Using the Dictionary

In order to be comfortable using a dictionary, your child must know how to alphabetize words effectively and also how to use *guide words*—those words at the top of a dictionary page that list the first and last word on each page. Using alphabetical order, if a word falls between these two guide words, it will be found on that page.

| newt | none |
|------|------|
|      |      |

In the sample dictionary page above, the guide words *newt* and *none* indicate that you would find the word *nine* on that page because it falls alphabetically between the two guide words. You would not find *never* because that comes before the word *newt,* which is the first word on that page.

In addition to guide words, your child should know what to find in a typical dictionary entry—the definition, the correct spelling, the correct pronunciation, and the number of syllables it has.

**busy** \'biz-e–\ 1. a. engaged in action. b. being in use.

From this entry, your child can learn that *busy* has two meanings, that it has two syllables, and that it is pronounced with a long *e*.

## What Third Graders Should Know

By third grade, your child should know what to find in a dictionary and how to find it. She should be able to use alphabetizing skills and guide words to locate any word she needs to find.

## What You and Your Child Can Do

**Play Word Coverup.** Open a dictionary and cover up all the words on the page except for the two guide words. Ask your child to come up with a word that she thinks is on the page (that would fit alphabetically between the two guide words). Uncover the page and see if the word is there.

**Ready … Set … Look It Up!** Get out your timer for this one. Write down a list of words of more than three letters. Give your child one word at a time, and set the timer to see how long it takes her to find the word. As her skill improves, use harder, more complex words. If you have more than one child, you can turn it into a competition and see who finds the word first.

**Model It.** If you come across a word you don't understand, make sure your child sees you going to the dictionary to look it up. Ask your child what she thinks the word means. Likewise, if your child is reading and comes

across a word she doesn't understand, don't just define it for her. Tell her to look it up, and follow through with her to make sure she does.

## What Tests May Ask

Standardized tests for this age will assess how well your child understands what a dictionary entry means and how to look up words. Tests may present a sample dictionary page and ask your child to tell which word may—or may not—fall within two given guide words. Tests also may ask where students should look to find the answers to certain questions.

## Practice Skill: Using the Dictionary

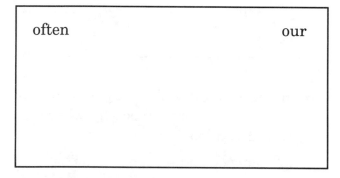

**Directions:** Which word would you find on the dictionary page above, between the guide words *often* and *our*?

**Example:**
- (A) off
- (B) of
- (C) ogle
- (D) igloo

**Answer:**
- (C) ogle

**4** Which word would you find between the guide words on the dictionary page above?

Ⓐ ouch

Ⓑ oats

Ⓒ oval

Ⓓ oxen

**5** Which word would you **not** find between the guide words on the dictionary page above?

Ⓐ omen

Ⓑ oblong

Ⓒ one

Ⓓ once

**6** If you wanted to find out how to pronounce the word <u>especially</u> where would you look?

Ⓐ encyclopedia

Ⓑ atlas

Ⓒ newspaper

Ⓓ dictionary

**7** What things could you **not** find in a dictionary?

Ⓐ how to pronounce a word

Ⓑ how many syllables a word has

Ⓒ what book is on the best seller list

Ⓓ what language the word came from

(See page 116 for answer key.)

## Reading Graphs

Learning how to read charts and graphs is another important aspect of study skills that will be introduced in third grade, and it may be taught in several different skill areas including language arts and mathematics. Bar graphs, line graphs, and picture graphs are typically discussed during this year.

## What Third Graders Should Know

Third graders should be comfortable working with different types of graphs, including picture graphs and bar graphs. They can create their own graphs and correctly gather information that others produce.

## What You and Your Child Can Do

**Graph It!** Graphs can be a fun way of measuring and categorizing lots of things around the house. Get several sheets of paper, and have your child design graphs to illustrate how many pairs of socks each member of the family has.

**Be a Weatherperson.** Get your child an inexpensive rain gauge, or make one from a plastic cup and a ruler. Have your child measure the rain for a week or a month, and graph the results. Temperature measurements and snow levels also work well.

## What Tests May Ask

Standardized tests will present a variety of different types of graphs and ask specific questions based on the information they contain. If your child has had lots of practice in interpreting graphs, these shouldn't be a surprise to her. Make sure she takes her time and studies the graphs carefully.

## Practice Skill: Reading Graphs

**Directions:** Look at the graph below. Choose the correct answer to each question.

Favorite Pizza Toppings in Our Class

bacon
pepperoni
cheese

**Example:**

What does this graph represent?

Ⓐ the number of pets in the class

Ⓑ the numbers of students who like certain pizza toppings

Ⓒ how many pizza toppings there are in the world

Ⓓ the number of students absent this week

**Answer:**

Ⓑ the number of students who like certain pizza toppings

---

**8** What does the gray bar represent?

Ⓐ bacon toppings

Ⓑ pepperoni toppings

Ⓒ anchovy toppings

Ⓓ cheese toppings

---

**9** What does the white bar represent?

Ⓐ bacon toppings

Ⓑ pepperoni toppings

Ⓒ anchovy toppings

Ⓓ cheese toppings

---

**10** What does the black bar represent?

Ⓐ bacon toppings

Ⓑ pepperoni toppings

Ⓒ anchovy toppings

Ⓓ cheese toppings

---

**11** How many students all together are represented in the chart?

Ⓐ 30

Ⓑ 10

Ⓒ 45

Ⓓ 5

---

(See page 116 for answer key.)

## Recognizing Parts of a Book

If students are going to do well in their educational career, they will need to have a thorough knowledge of how to find information in a book. They need to know what kind of information is included in the title page, table of contents, glossary, and index.

## What Third Graders Should Know

Your third grader should know that the title page contains the title of the book and the author's name, plus the name of the publisher and where the book was published. She should know that a table of contents tells her what information will be contained in the book and (usually) on what page the chapters begin. The bibliography reveals what other resources the author used to write the book, and the glossary is a sort of minidictionary that may give the definitions of some of the terms used in the book. Finally, the index is the place to go to find the exact page number for every term or fact cited in the book.

## What You and Your Child Can Do

**Make a Publisher Chart.** Set your child on a scavenger hunt. Armed with a pen and piece of paper, send her to the bookshelf to make a list of five different publishers and the names of their books and where the books were published. If your child likes this sort of activity, ask her to locate 10 or 15. Keep a chart, and see if she notices the types of books that any one publisher specializes in.

**Make Your Own Book.** One of the best ways to teach your child about different parts of a book is to help her make her own, complete with table of contents and index. Have her number the pages so that she can create an index.

**Play Wordfind.** Teach your child the correct use of an index. Find a simple nonfiction book with a good index. Make a list of 10 terms that are listed in the index. Set the timer, and call out the terms for her to locate in the book.

## What Tests May Ask

Standardized tests will ask specific questions about the types of information that can be found in different parts of a book, or where a reader would go to find certain information.

## Practice Skill: Parts of a Book

**Directions:** Choose the correct answer for each of the following questions.

**Example:**

Where would you look to find detailed information on the life and times of Albert Einstein?

- Ⓐ encyclopedia
- Ⓑ dictionary
- Ⓒ poetry book
- Ⓓ atlas

**Answer:**

- Ⓐ encyclopedia

12  If Kara wanted to find out the definition of <u>kennel cough</u> in her book on show dogs, where would she look?

- Ⓐ index
- Ⓑ table of contents
- Ⓒ title page
- Ⓓ glossary

13  If you are reading a book about baseball players and you want to find the page that contains a specific statistic, where would you look to find that page number?

- Ⓐ in the table of contents
- Ⓑ in the glossary
- Ⓒ in the index
- Ⓓ in the title page

14  Georgia wants to get a general idea of the topics covered in her book on stamps. She would look in

- Ⓐ the table of contents.
- Ⓑ the glossary.
- Ⓒ the index.
- Ⓓ the title page.

(See page 116 for answer key.)

# Web Sites and Resources for More Information

## Homework

### Homework Central
http://www.HomeworkCentral.com
Terrific site for students, parents, and teachers, filled with information, projects, and more.

### Win the Homework Wars
(Sylvan Learning Centers)
http://www.educate.com/online/qa_peters.html

## Reading and Grammar Help

### Born to Read: How to Raise a Reader
http://www.ala.org/alsc/raise_a_reader.html

### Guide to Grammar and Writing
http://webster.commnet.edu/hp/pages/darling/grammar.htm
Help with "plague words and phrases," grammar FAQs, sentence parts, punctuation, rules for common usage.

### Internet Public Library: Reading Zone
http://www.ipl.org/cgi-bin/youth/youth.out

### Keeping Kids Reading and Writing
http://www.tiac.net/users/maryl/

### U.S. Dept. of Education: Helping Your Child Learn to Read
http://www.ed.gov/pubs/parents/Reading/index.html

## Math Help

### Center for Advancement of Learning
http://www.muskingum.edu/%7Ecal/database/Math2.html
Substitution and memory strategies for math.

### Center for Advancement of Learning
http://www.muskingum.edu/%7Ecal/database/Math1.html
General tips and suggestions.

### Math.com
http://www.math.com
The world of math online.

### Math.com
http://www.math.com/student/testprep.html
Get ready for standardized tests.

### Math.com: Homework Help in Math
http://www.math.com/students/homework.html

### Math.com: Math for Homeschoolers
http://www.math.com/parents/homeschool.html

### The Math Forum: Problems and Puzzles
http://forum.swarthmore.edu/library/resource_types/problems_puzzles
Lots of fun math puzzles and problems for grades K through 12.

### The Math Forum: Math Tips and Tricks
http://forum.swarthmore.edu/k12/mathtips/mathtips.html

## Tips on Testing

### Books on Test Preparation
http://www.testbooksonline.com/preHS.asp
This site provides printed resources for parents who wish to help their children prepare for standardized school tests.

### Core Knowledge Web Site
http://www.coreknowledge.org/
Site dedicated to providing resources for parents; based on the books of E. D. Hirsch, Jr., who wrote the *What Your X Grader Needs to Know* series.

### Family Education Network
http://www.familyeducation.com/article/0,1120,
1-6219,00.html
This report presents some of the arguments against current standardized testing practices in the public schools. The site also provides links to family activities that help kids learn.

### Math.com
http://www.math.com/students/testprep.html
Get ready for standardized tests.

### Standardized Tests
http://arc.missouri.edu/k12/
K through 12 assessment tools and know-how.

## Parents: Testing in Schools

### KidSource: Talking to Your Child's Teacher about Standardized Tests
http://www.kidsource.com/kidsource/content2/
talking.assessment.k12.4.html
This site provides basic information to help parents understand their children's test results and provides pointers for how to discuss the results with their children's teachers.

### eSCORE.com: State Test and Education Standards
http://www.eSCORE.com
Find out if your child meets the necessary requirements for your local schools. A Web site with experts from Brazelton Institute and Harvard's Project Zero.

### Overview of States' Assessment Programs
http://ericae.net/faqs/

### Parent Soup
### Education Central: Standardized Tests
http://www.parentsoup.com/edcentral/testing
A parent's guide to standardized testing in the schools, written from a parent advocacy standpoint.

### National Center for Fair and Open Testing, Inc. (FairTest)
342 Broadway
Cambridge, MA 02139
(617) 864-4810
http://www.fairtest.org

### National Parent Information Network
http://npin.org

### Publications for Parents from the U.S. Department of Education
http://www.ed.gov/pubs/parents/
An ever-changing list of information for parents available from the U.S. Department of Education.

### State of the States Report
http://www.edweek.org/sreports/qc99/states/
indicators/in-intro.htm
A report on testing and achievement in the 50 states.

## Testing: General Information

### Academic Center for Excellence
http://www.acekids.com

### American Association for Higher Education Assessment
http://www.aahe.org/assessment/web.htm

### American Educational Research Association (AERA)
http://aera.net
An excellent link to reports on American education, including reports on the controversy over standardized testing.

### American Federation of Teachers
555 New Jersey Avenue, NW
Washington, D.C. 20011

**Association of Test Publishers Member Products and Services**
http://www.testpublishers.org/memserv.htm

**Education Week on the Web**
http://www.edweek.org

**ERIC Clearinghouse on Assessment and Evaluation**
1131 Shriver Lab
University of Maryland
College Park, MD 20742
http://ericae.net
A clearinghouse of information on assessment and education reform.

**FairTest: The National Center for Fair and Open Testing**
http://fairtest.org/facts/ntfact.htm
http://fairtest.org/
The National Center for Fair and Open Testing is an advocacy organization working to end the abuses, misuses, and flaws of standardized testing and to ensure that evaluation of students and workers is fair, open, and educationally sound. This site provides many links to fact sheets, opinion papers, and other sources of information about testing.

**National Congress of Parents and Teachers**
700 North Rush Street
Chicago, Illinois 60611

**National Education Association**
1201 16th Street, NW
Washington, DC 20036

**National School Boards Association**
http://www.nsba.org
A good source for information on all aspects of public education, including standardized testing.

**Testing Our Children: A Report Card on State Assessment Systems**
http://www.fairtest.org/states/survey.htm
Report of testing practices of the states, with graphical links to the states and a critique of fair testing practices in each state.

**Trends in Statewide Student Assessment Programs: A Graphical Summary**
http://www.ccsso.org/survey96.html
Results of annual survey of states' departments of public instruction regarding their testing practices.

**U.S. Department of Education**
http://www.ed.gov/

**Web Links for Parents Who Want to Help Their Children Achieve**
http://www.liveandlearn.com/learn.html
This page offers many Web links to free and for-sale information and materials for parents who want to help their children do well in school. Titles include such free offerings as the Online Colors Game and questionnaires to determine whether your child is ready for school.

**What Should Parents Know about Standardized Testing in the Schools?**
http://www.rusd.k12.ca.us/parents/standard.html
An online brochure about standardized testing in the schools, with advice regarding how to become an effective advocate for your child.

**Test Publishers Online**

**ACT: Information for Life's Transitions**
http://www.act.org

**American Guidance Service, Inc.**
http://www.agsnet.com

**Ballard & Tighe Publishers**
http://www.ballard-tighe.com

**Consulting Psychologists Press**
http://www.cpp-db.com

**CTB McGraw-Hill**
http://www.ctb.com

**Educational Records Bureau**
http://www.erbtest.org/index.html

**Educational Testing Service**
http://www.ets.org

**General Educational Development (GED) Testing Service**
http://www.acenet.edu/calec/ged/home.html

**Harcourt Brace Educational Measurement**
http://www.hbem.com

**Piney Mountain Press—A Cyber-Center for Career and Applied Learning**
http://www.pineymountain.com

**ProEd Publishing**
http://www.proedinc.com

**Riverside Publishing Company**
http://www.hmco.com/hmco/riverside

**Stoelting Co.**
http://www.stoeltingco.com

**Sylvan Learning Systems, Inc.**
http://www.educate.com

**Touchstone Applied Science Associates, Inc. (TASA)**
http://www.tasa.com

**Tests Online**

(*Note:* We don't endorse tests; some may not have technical documentation. Evaluate the quality of any testing program before making decisions based on its use.)

**Edutest, Inc.**
http://www.edutest.com
Edutest is an Internet-accessible testing service that offers criterion-referenced tests for elementary school students, based upon the standards for K through 12 learning and achievement in the states of Virginia, California, and Florida.

**Virtual Knowledge**
http://www.smarterkids.com
This commercial service, which enjoys a formal partnership with Sylvan Learning Centers, offers a line of skills assessments for preschool through grade 9 for use in the classroom or the home. For free online sample tests, see the Virtual Test Center.

# Read More about It

Abbamont, Gary W. *Test Smart: Ready-to-Use Test-Taking Strategies and Activities for Grades 5–12*. Upper Saddle River, NJ: Prentice Hall Direct, 1997.

Cookson, Peter W., and Joshua Halberstam. *A Parent's Guide to Standardized Tests in School: How to Improve Your Child's Chances for Success*. New York: Learning Express, 1998.

Frank, Steven, and Stephen Frank. *Test-Taking Secrets: Study Better, Test Smarter, and Get Great Grades (The Backpack Study Series)*. Holbrook, MA: Adams Media Corporation, 1998.

Gilbert, Sara Dulaney. *How to Do Your Best on Tests: A Survival Guide*. New York: Beech Tree Books, 1998.

Gruber, Gary. *Dr. Gary Gruber's Essential Guide to Test-Taking for Kids, Grades 3–5*. New York: William Morrow & Co., 1986.

———. *Gary Gruber's Essential Guide to Test-Taking for Kids, Grades 6, 7, 8, 9*. New York: William Morrow & Co., 1997.

Leonhardt, Mary. *99 Ways to Get Kids to Love Reading and 100 Books They'll Love*. New York: Crown, 1997.

———. *Parents Who Love Reading, Kids Who Don't: How It Happens and What You Can Do about It*. New York: Crown, 1995.

McGrath, Barbara B. *The Baseball Counting Book*. Watertown, MA: Charlesbridge, 1999.

———. *More M&M's Brand Chocolate Candies Math*. Watertown, MA: Charlesbridge, 1998.

Mokros, Janice R. *Beyond Facts & Flashcards: Exploring Math with Your Kids*. Portsmouth, NH: Heinemann, 1996.

Romain, Trevor, and Elizabeth Verdick. *True or False?: Tests Stink!* Minneapolis: Free Spirit Publishing Co., 1999.

Schartz, Eugene M. *How to Double Your Child's Grades in School: Build Brilliance and Leadership into Your Child—from Kindergarten to College—in Just 5 Minutes a Day*. New York: Barnes & Noble, 1999.

Taylor, Kathe, and Sherry Walton. *Children at the Center: A Workshop Approach to Standardized Test Preparation, K–8*. Portsmouth, NH: Heinemann, 1998.

Tobia, Sheila. *Overcoming Math Anxiety*. New York: W. W. Norton & Company, Inc., 1995.

Tufariello, Ann Hunt. *Up Your Grades: Proven Strategies for Academic Success*. Lincolnwood, IL: VGM Career Horizons, 1996.

Vorderman, Carol. *How Math Works*. Pleasantville, NY: Reader's Digest Association, Inc., 1996.

Zahler, Kathy A. *50 Simple Things You Can Do to Raise a Child Who Loves to Read*. New York: IDG Books, 1997.

# What Your Child's Test Scores Mean

Several weeks or months after your child has taken standardized tests, you will receive a report such as the TerraNova Home Report found in Figures 1 and 2. You will receive similar reports if your child has taken other tests. We briefly examine what information the reports include.

Look at the first page of the Home Report. Note that the chart provides labeled bars showing the child's performance. Each bar is labeled with the child's National Percentile for that skill area. When you know how to interpret them, national percentiles can be the most useful scores you encounter on reports such as this. Even when you are confronted with different tests that use different scale scores, you can always interpret percentiles the same way, regardless of the test. A percentile tells the percent of students who score at or below that level. A percentile of 25, for example, means that 25 percent of children taking the test scored at or below that score. (It also means that 75 percent of students scored above that score.) Note that the average is always at the 50th percentile.

On the right side of the graph on the first page of the report, the publisher has designated the ranges of scores that constitute average, above average, and below average. You can also use this slightly more precise key for interpreting percentiles:

| PERCENTILE RANGE | LEVEL |
|---|---|
| 2 and Below | Deficient |
| 3–8 | Borderline |
| 9–23 | Low Average |
| 24–75 | Average |
| 76–97 | High Average |
| 98 and Up | Superior |

The second page of the Home report provides a listing of the child's strengths and weaknesses, along with keys for mastery, partial mastery, and non-mastery of the skills. Scoring services determine these breakdowns based on the child's scores as compared with those from the national norm group.

Your child's teacher or guidance counselor will probably also receive a profile report similar to the TerraNova Individual Profile Report, shown in Figures 3 and 4. That report will be kept in your child's permanent record. The first aspect of this report to notice is that the scores are expressed both numerically and graphically.

First look at the score bands under National Percentile. Note that the scores are expressed as bands, with the actual score represented by a dot within each band. The reason we express the scores as bands is to provide an idea of the amount by which typical scores may vary for each student. That is, each band represents a

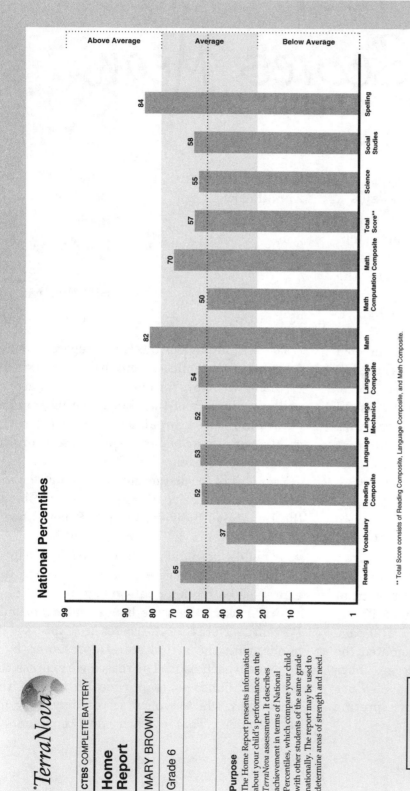

**Figure 1** (SOURCE: CTB/McGraw-Hill, copyright © 1997. All rights reserved. Reproduced with permission.)

*TerraNova*

CTBS COMPLETE BATTERY

## Home Report

MARY BROWN

Grade 6

**Purpose**

This page of the Home Report presents information about your child's strengths and needs. This information is provided to help you monitor your child's academic growth.

---

Simulated Data

Birthdate: 02/08/85
Special Codes:
A B C D E F G H I J K L M N O P Q R S T
3 5 9 7 3 2           1 1 1
Form/Level: A-16
Test Date: 11/01/99    Scoring: PATTERN (IRT)
QM: 08                 Norms Date: 1996

Class: PARKER
School: WINFIELD
District: WINFIELD

City/State: WINFIELD, CA

**CTB McGraw-Hill**  *Page 2*   Copyright © 1997 CTB/McGraw-Hill. All rights reserved.

---

## Strengths

**Reading**
● Basic Understanding
● Analyze Text

**Vocabulary**
● Word Meaning
● Words in Context

**Language**
● Editing Skills
● Sentence Structure

**Language Mechanics**
● Sentences, Phrases, Clauses

**Mathematics**
● Computation and Numerical Estimation
● Operation Concepts

**Mathematics Computation**
● Add Whole Numbers
● Multiply Whole Numbers

**Science**
● Life Science
● Inquiry Skills

**Social Studies**
● Geographic Perspectives
● Economic Perspectives

**Spelling**
● Vowels
● Consonants

Key  ● **Mastery**

## General Interpretation

The left column shows your child's best areas of performance. In each case, your child has reached mastery level. The column at the right shows the areas within each test section where your child's scores are the lowest. In these cases, your child has not reached mastery level, although he or she may have reached partial mastery.

---

## Needs

**Reading**
◐ Evaluate and Extend Meaning
○ Identify Reading Strategies

**Vocabulary**
○ Multimeaning Words

**Language**
◐ Writing Strategies

**Language Mechanics**
○ Writing Conventions

**Mathematics**
◐ Measurement
○ Geometry and Spatial Sense

**Mathematics Computation**
○ Percents

**Science**
○ Earth and Space Science

**Social Studies**
◐ Historical and Cultural Perspectives

**Spelling**
No area of needs were identified for this content area

Key  ◐ **Partial Mastery**   ○ **Non-Mastery**

---

**Figure 2**  (SOURCE: CTB/McGraw-Hill, copyright © 1997. All rights reserved. Reproduced with permission.)

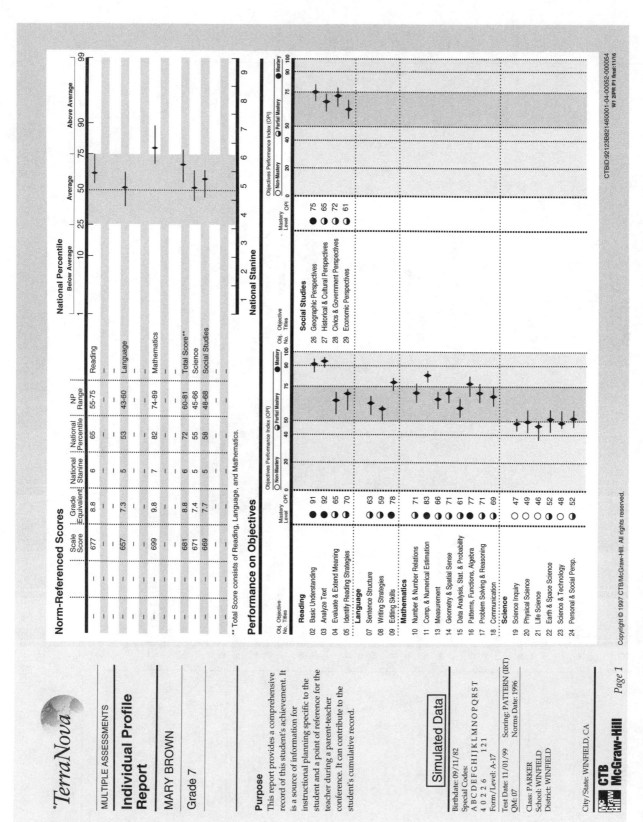

**Figure 3** (SOURCE: CTB/McGraw-Hill, copyright © 1997. All rights reserved. Reproduced with permission.)

## Observations

### Norm-Referenced Scores

The top section of the report presents information about this student's achievement in several different ways. The National Percentile (NP) data and graph indicate how this student performed compared to students of the same grade nationally. The National Percentile range indicates that if this student had taken the test numerous times the scores would have fallen within the range shown. The shaded area on the graph represents the average range of scores, usually defined as the middle 50 percent of students nationally. Scores in the area to the right of the shading are above the average range. Scores in the area to the left of the shading are below the average range.

In Reading, for example, this student achieved a National Percentile rank of 65. This student scored higher than 65 percent of the students nationally. This score is in the average range. This student has a total of five scores in the average range. One score is in the above average range. No scores are in the below average range.

### Performance on Objectives

The next section of the report presents performance on the objectives. Each objective is measured by a minimum of 4 items. The Objectives Performance Index (OPI) provides an estimate of the number of items that a student could be expected to answer correctly if there had been 100 items for that objective. The OPI is used to indicate mastery of each objective. An OPI of 75 and above characterizes Mastery. An OPI between 50 and 74 indicates Partial Mastery, and an OPI below 50 indicates Non-Mastery. The two-digit number preceding the objective title identifies the objective, which is fully described in the Teacher's Guide to *TerraNova*. The bands on either side of the diamonds indicate the range within which the student's test scores would fall if the student were tested numerous times.

In Reading, for example, this student could be expected to respond correctly to 91 out of 100 items measuring Basic Understanding. If this student had taken the test numerous times the OPI for this objective would have fallen between 82 and 93.

## Teacher Notes

*TerraNova*

MULTIPLE ASSESSMENTS

## Individual Profile Report

MARY BROWN

Grade 7

### Purpose

The Observations section of the Individual Profile Report gives teachers and parents information to interpret this report. This page is a narrative description of the data on the other side.

Simulated Data

Birthdate: 09/11/82
Special Codes:
A B C D E F G H I J K L M N O P Q R S T
4 0 2 2 6      1 2 1
Form/Level: A-17

Test Date: 11/01/99     Scoring: PATTERN (IRT)
QM: 08                  Norms Date: 1996

Class: PARKER
School: WINFIELD
District: WINFIELD

City/State: WINFIELD, CA

CTB
McGraw-Hill

*Page 2*

CTBID:9212388821460001-04-0052-000054
W1 IPR P2 final:11/05

**Figure 4** (SOURCE: CTB/McGraw-Hill, copyright © 1997. All rights reserved. Reproduced with permission.)

*TerraNova*

MULTIPLE ASSESSMENTS

**Student Performance Level Report**

KEN ALLEN

Grade 4

**Purpose**

This report describes this student's achievement in terms of five performance levels for each content area. The meaning of these levels is described on the back of this page. Performance levels are a new way of describing achievement.

| Simulated Data |
| --- |

Birthdate: 02/08/86
Special Codes:
A B C D E F G H I J K L M N O P Q R S T
3 5 9 7 3 2     1 1 1
Form/Level: A-14

Test Date: 04/15/97    Scoring: PATTERN (IRT)
QM: 31            Norms Date: 1996

Class: SCHWARZ
School: WINFIELD
District: GREEN VALLEY

City/State: WINFIELD, CA

**CTB McGraw-Hill**

*Page 1*

| Performance Levels | Reading | Language | Mathematics | Science | Social Studies |
| --- | --- | --- | --- | --- | --- |
| **5** Advanced | | | | | |
| **4** Proficient | | | | | |
| **3** Nearing Proficiency | ✓ | ✓ | ✓ | | ✓ |
| **2** Progressing | ✓ | ✓ | ✓ | ✓ | ✓ |
| **1** Step 1 | ✓ | ✓ | ✓ | ✓ | ✓ |

Partially Proficient

**Observations**

Performance level scores provide a measure of what students *can do* in terms of the content and skills assessed by *TerraNova*, and typically found in curricula for Grades 3, 4, and 5. It is desirable to work towards achieving a Level 4 (Proficient) or Level 5 (Advanced) by the end of Grade 5.

The number of check marks indicates the performance level this student reached in each content area. For example, this student reached Level 3 in Reading and Social Studies.

The performance level indicates this student can perform the majority of what is described for that level and even more of what is described for the levels below. The student may also be capable of performing some of the things described in the next higher level, but not enough to have reached that level of performance.

For example, this student can perform the majority of what is described for Level 3 in Reading and even more of what is described for Level 2 and Level 1 in Reading. This student may also be capable of performing some of what is described for Level 4 in Reading.

For each content area look at the skills and knowledge described in the next higher level. These are the competencies this student needs to demonstrate to show academic growth.

**Figure 5** (SOURCE: CTB/McGraw-Hill, copyright © 1997. All rights reserved. Reproduced with permission.)

| Performance Levels (Grades 3, 4, 5) | Reading | Language | Mathematics | Science | Social Studies |
|---|---|---|---|---|---|
| **5** Advanced | Students use analogies to generalize. They identify a paraphrase of concepts or ideas in texts. They can indicate thought processes that led them to a previous answer. In written responses, they demonstrate understanding of an implied theme, assess intent of passage information, and provide justification as well as support for their answers. | Students understand logical development in paragraph structure. They identify essential information from notes. They recognize the effect of prepositional phrases on subject-verb agreement. They find and correct at least 4 out of 6 errors when editing simple narratives. They correct run-on and incomplete sentences in more complex texts. They can eliminate all errors when editing their own work. | Students locate decimals on a number line; compute with decimals and fractions; read scale drawings; find areas; identify geometric transformations; construct and label bar graphs; find simple probabilities; find averages; use patterns in data to solve problems; use multiple strategies and concepts to solve unfamiliar problems; express mathematical ideas and explain the problem-solving process. | Students understand a broad range of grade level scientific concepts, such as the structure of Earth and instinctive behavior. They know terminology, such as decomposers; fossil fuel, eclipse, and buoyancy. Knowledge of more complex environmental issues includes, for example, the positive consequences of a forest fire. Students can process and interpret more detailed tables and graphs. They can suggest improvements to experimental design, such as running more trials. | Students consistently demonstrate skills such as synthesizing information from two sources (e.g., a document and a map). They show understanding of the democratic process and global environmental issues, and know the location of continents and major countries. They analyze and summarize information from multiple sources in early American history. They thoroughly explain both sides of an issue and give complete and detailed written answers to questions. |
| **4** Proficient | Students interpret figures of speech. They recognize paraphrase of text information and retrieve information to complete forms. In more complex texts, they identify themes, main ideas, or author purpose/point of view. They analyze and apply information in graphic and text form, make reasonable generalizations, and draw conclusions. In written responses, they can identify key elements from text. | Students select the best supporting sentences for a topic sentence. They use compound predicates to combine sentences. They identify simple subjects and predicates, recognize correct usage when confronted with two types of errors, and find and correct at least 3 out of 6 errors when editing simple narratives. They can edit their own work with only minor errors. | Students compare, order, and round whole numbers; know place value to thousands; identify fractions; use computation and estimation strategies; relate multiplication to addition; measure to nearest half-inch and centimeter; estimate measures; find perimeters; measure and find elapsed times; combine and subdivide shapes; identify parallel lines; interpret tables and graphs; solve two-step problems. | Students have a range of specific science knowledge, including details about animal adaptations and classification, states of matter, and the geology of Earth. They recognize scientific words such as habitat, gravity, and mass. They understand the usefulness of computers and natural resources. Understanding of experimentation includes analyzing purpose, interpreting data, and selecting tools to gather data. | Students demonstrate skills such as making inferences, using historical documents and analyzing maps to determine the economic strengths of a region. They understand the function of currency in various cultures and supply and demand. They summarize information from multiple sources, recognize relationships, determine relevance of information, and show global awareness. They propose solutions to real-world problems and support ideas with appropriate details. |
| **3** Nearing Proficiency | Students use context clues and structural analysis to determine word meaning. They recognize homonyms and antonyms in grade-level text. They identify important details, sequence, cause and effect, and lessons embedded in the text. They interpret characters' feelings and apply information to new situations. In written responses, they can express an opinion and support it. | Students identify irrelevant sentences in paragraphs and select the best place to add new information. They recognize faulty sentence construction. They can combine simple sentences with conjunctions and use simple subordination of phrases/clauses. They identify reference sources. They recognize correct conventions for dates, closings, and place names in informal correspondence. | Students identify even and odd numbers; subtract whole numbers with regrouping; multiply and divide by one-digit numbers; identify simple fractions; measure with ruler to nearest inch; tell time to nearest fifteen minutes; recognize and classify common shapes; recognize symmetry; subdivide shapes; complete bar graphs; extend numerical and geometric patterns; apply simple logical reasoning. | Students are familiar with the life cycles of plants and animals. They can identify an example of a cold-blooded animal. They infer what once existed from fossil evidence. They recognize the term habitat. They understand the water cycle. They know science and society issues such as recycling and sources of pollution. They can sequence technological advances. They extrapolate data, devise a simple classification scheme, and determine the purpose of a simple experiment. | Students demonstrate skills in organizing information. They use time lines, product and global maps, and cardinal directions. They understand simple cause and effect relationships and historical documents. They sequence events, associate holidays with events, and classify natural resources. They compare life in different times and understand some economic concepts related to products, jobs, and the environment. They give some detail in written responses. |
| **2** Progressing | Students identify synonyms for grade-level words, and use context clues to define common words. They make simple inferences and predictions based on text. They identify characters' feelings. They can transfer information from text to graphic form, or from graphic form to text. In written responses, they can provide limited support for their answers. | Students identify the use of correct verb tenses and supply verbs to complete sentences. They complete paragraphs by selecting an appropriate topic sentence. They edit for the correct use of pronouns. They select correct adjective forms. | Students know ordinal numbers; solve coin combination problems; count by tens; add whole numbers with regrouping; have basic estimation skills; understand addition property of zero; write and identify number sentences describing simple situations; read calendars; identify appropriate measurement tools; recognize congruent figures; use simple coordinate grids; read common tables and graphs. | Students recognize that plants decompose and become part of soil. They can classify a plant as a vegetable. They recognize that camouflage relates to survival. They recognize terms such as hibernate. They have an understanding of human impact on the environment and are familiar with causes of pollution. They find the correct bar graph to represent given data and transfer data appropriate for middle elementary grades to a bar graph. | Students demonstrate simple information-processing skills such as using basic maps and keys. They recognize simple geographical terms, types of jobs, modes of transportation, and natural resources. They connect a human need with an appropriate community service. They identify some early famous presidents and know the capital of the United States. Their written answers are partially complete. |
| **1** Step 1 | Students select pictured representations of ideas and identify stated details contained in simple texts. In written responses, they can select and transfer information from charts. | Students supply subjects to complete sentences. They identify the correct use of pronouns. They edit for the correct use of end marks and initial capital letters, and identify the correct convention for greetings in letters. | Students read and recognize numbers to 1000; identify real-world use of numbers; add and subtract two-digit numbers without regrouping; identify addition situations; recognize and complete simple geometric and numerical patterns. | Students recognize basic adaptations for living in the water, identify an animal that is hatched from an egg, and associate an organism with its correct environment. They identify an object as metal. They have some understanding of conditions on the moon. They supply one way a computer can be useful. They associate an instrument like a telescope with a field of study. | Students are developing fundamental social studies skills such as locating and classifying basic information. They locate information in pictures and read and complete simple bar graphs related to social studies concepts and contexts. They can connect some city buildings with their functions and recognize certain historical objects. |

Partially Proficient

IMPORTANT: Each performance level, depicted on the other side, indicates the student can perform the majority of what is described for that level and even more of what is described for the levels below. The student may also be capable of performing some of the things described in the next higher level, but not enough to have reached that level.

**Figure 6** (Source: CTB/McGraw-Hill, copyright © 1997. All rights reserved. Reproduced with permission.)

*confidence interval.* In these reports, we usually report either a 90 percent or 95 percent confidence interval. Interpret a confidence interval this way: Suppose we report a 90 percent confidence interval of 25 to 37. This means we estimate that, if the child took the test multiple times, we would expect that child's score to be in the 25 to 37 range 90 percent of the time.

Now look under the section titled Norm-Referenced Scores on the first page of the Individual Profile Report (Figure 3). The farthest column on the right provides the NP Range, which is the National Percentile scores represented by the score bands in the chart.

Next notice the column labeled Grade Equivalent. Theoretically, grade level equivalents equate a student's score in a skill area with the average grade placement of children who made the same score. Many psychologists and test developers would prefer that we stopped reporting grade equivalents, because they can be grossly misleading. For example, the average reading grade level of high school seniors as reported by one of the more popular tests is the eighth grade level. Does that mean that the nation's high school seniors cannot read? No. The way the test publisher calculated grade equivalents was to determine the average test scores for students in grades 4 to 6 and then simply extend the resulting prediction formula to grades 7 to 12. The result is that parents of average high school seniors who take the test in question would mistakenly believe that their seniors are reading four grade levels behind! Stick to the percentile in interpreting your child's scores.

Now look at the columns labeled Scale Score and National Stanine. These are two of a group of scores we also call *standard scores.* In reports for other tests, you may see other standard scores reported, such as Normal Curve Equivalents (NCEs), Z-Scores, and T-Scores. The IQ that we report on intelligence tests, for example, is a standard score. Standard scores are simply a way of expressing a student's scores in terms of the statistical properties of the scores from the norm group against which we are comparing the child. Although most psychologists prefer to speak in terms of standard scores among themselves, parents are advised to stick to percentiles in interpreting your child's performance.

Now look at the section of the report labeled Performance on Objectives. In this section, the test publisher reports how your child did on the various skills that make up each skills area. Note that the scores on each objective are expressed as a percentile band, and you are again told whether your child's score constitutes mastery, non-mastery, or partial mastery. Note that these scores are made up of tallies of sometimes small numbers of test items taken from sections such as Reading or Math. Because they are calculated from a much smaller number of scores than the main scales are (for example, Sentence Comprehension is made up of fewer items than overall Reading), their scores are less reliable than those of the main scales.

Now look at the second page of the Individual Profile Report (Figure 4). Here the test publisher provides a narrative summary of how the child did on the test. These summaries are computer-generated according to rules provided by the publisher. Note that the results descriptions are more general than those on the previous three report pages. But they allow the teacher to form a general picture of which students are performing at what general skill levels.

Finally, your child's guidance counselor may receive a summary report such as the TerraNova Student Performance Level Report. (See Figures 5 and 6.) In this report, the publisher explains to school personnel what skills the test assessed and generally how proficiently the child tested under each skill.

# Which States Require Which Tests

Tables 1 through 3 summarize standardized testing practices in the 50 states and the District of Columbia. This information is constantly changing; the information presented here was accurate as of the date of printing of this book. Many states have changed their testing practices in response to revised accountability legislation, while others have changed the tests they use.

**Table 1**  State Web Sites: Education and Testing

| STATE | GENERAL WEB SITE | STATE TESTING WEB SITE |
|---|---|---|
| Alabama | http://www.alsde.edu/ | http://www.fairtest.org/states/al.htm |
| Alaska | www.educ.state.ak.us/ | http://www.educ.state.ak.us/ |
| Arizona | http://www.ade.state.az.us/ | http://www.ade.state.az.us/standards/ |
| Arkansas | http://arkedu.k12.ar.us/ | http://www.fairtest.org/states/ar.htm |
| California | http://goldmine.cde.ca.gov/ | http://star.cde.ca.gov/ |
| Colorado | http://www.cde.state.co.us/index_home.htm | http://www.cde.state.co.us/index_assess.htm |
| Connecticut | http://www.state.ct.us/sde/ | http://www.state.ct.us/sde/cmt/index.htm |
| Delaware | http://www.doe.state.de.us/ | http://www.doe.state.de.us/aab/index.htm |
| District of Columbia | http://www.k12.dc.us/dcps/home.html | http://www.k12.dc.us/dcps/data/data_frame2.html |
| Florida | http://www.firn.edu/doe/ | http://www.firn.edu/doe/sas/sasshome.htm |
| Georgia | http://www.doe.k12.ga.us/ | http://www.doe.k12.ga.us/sla/ret/recotest.html |
| Hawaii | http://kalama.doe.hawaii.edu/upena/ | http://www.fairtest.org/states/hi.htm |
| Idaho | http://www.sde.state.id.us/Dept/ | http://www.sde.state.id.us/instruct/schoolaccount/statetesting.htm |
| Illinois | http://www.isbe.state.il.us/ | http://www.isbe.state.il.us/isat/ |
| Indiana | http://doe.state.in.us/ | http://doe.state.in.us/assessment/welcome.html |
| Iowa | http://www.state.ia.us/educate/index.html | (Tests Chosen Locally) |
| Kansas | http://www.ksbe.state.ks.us/ | http://www.ksbe.state.ks.us/assessment/ |
| Kentucky | htp://www.kde.state.ky.us/ | http://www.kde.state.ky.us/oaa/ |
| Louisiana | http://www.doe.state.la.us/DOE/asps/home.asp | http://www.doe.state.la.us/DOE/asps/home.asp?I=HISTAKES |
| Maine | http://janus.state.me.us/education/homepage.htm | http://janus.state.me.us/education/mea/meacompass.htm |
| Maryland | http://www.msde.state.md.us/ | http://msp.msde.state.md.us/ |
| Massachusetts | http://www.doe.mass.edu/ | http://www.doe.mass.edu/mcas/ |
| Michigan | http://www.mde.state.mi.us/ | http://www.MeritAward.state.mi.us/merit/meap/index.htm |

| STATE | GENERAL WEB SITE | STATE TESTING WEB SITE |
|-------|------------------|------------------------|
| Minnesota | http://www.educ.state.mn.us/ | http://fairtest.org/states/mn.htm |
| Mississippi | http://mdek12.state.ms.us/ | http://fairtest.org/states/ms.htm |
| Missouri | http://services.dese.state.mo.us/ | http://fairtest.org/states/mo.htm |
| Montana | http://www.metnet.state.mt.us/ | http://fairtest.org/states/mt.htm |
| Nebraska | http://www.nde.state.ne.us/ | http://www.edneb.org/IPS/AppAccrd/ApprAccrd.html |
| Nevada | http://www.nde.state.nv.us/ | http://www.nsn.k12.nv.us/nvdoe/reports/TerraNova.doc |
| New Hampshire | http://www.state.nh.us/doe/ | http://www.state.nh.us/doe/Assessment/assessme(NHEIAP).htm |
| New Jersey | http://www.state.nj.us/education/ | http://www.state.nj.us/njded/stass/index.html |
| New Mexico | http://sde.state.nm.us/ | http://sde.state.nm.us/press/august30a.html |
| New York | http://www.nysed.gov/ | http://www.emsc.nysed.gov/ciai/assess.html |
| North Carolina | http://www.dpi.state.nc.us/ | http://www.dpi.state.nc.us/accountability/reporting/index.html |
| North Dakota | http://www.dpi.state.nd.us/dpi/index.htm | http://www.dpi.state.nd.us/dpi/reports/assess/assess.htm |
| Ohio | http://www.ode.state.oh.us/ | http://www.ode.state.oh.us/ca/ |
| Oklahoma | http://sde.state.ok.us/ | http://sde.state.ok.us/acrob/testpack.pdf |
| Oregon | http://www.ode.state.or.us// | http://www.ode.state.or.us//asmt/index.htm |
| Pennsylvania | http://www.pde.psu.edu/ | http://www.fairtest.org/states/pa.htm |
| Rhode Island | http://www.ridoe.net/ | http://www.ridoe.net/standards/default.htm |
| South Carolina | http://www.state.sc.us/sde/ | http://www.state.sc.us/sde/reports/terranov.htm |
| South Dakota | http://www.state.sd.us/state/executive/deca/ | http://www.state.sd.us/state/executive/deca/TA/McRelReport/McRelReports.htm |
| Tennessee | http://www.state.tn.us/education/ | http://www.state.tn.us/education/tsintro.htm |
| Texas | http://www.tea.state.tx.us/ | http://www.tea.state.tx.us/student.assessment/ |
| Utah | http://www.usoe.k12.ut.us/ | http://www.usoe.k12.ut.us/eval/usoeeval.htm |
| Vermont | http://www.state.vt.us/educ/ | http://www.fairtest.org/states/vt.htm |

| STATE | GENERAL WEB SITE | STATE TESTING WEB SITE |
|---|---|---|
| Virginia | http://www.pen.k12.va.us/Anthology/VDOE/ | http://www.pen.k12.va.us/VDOE/Assessment/home.shtml |
| Washington | http://www.k12.wa.us/ | http://www.k12.wa.us/assessment/ |
| West Virginia | http://wvde.state.wv.us/ | http://wvde.state.wv.us/ |
| Wisconsin | http://www.dpi.state.wi.us/ | http://www.dpi.state.wi.us/dpi/dltcl/eis/achfacts.html |
| Wyoming | http://www.k12.wy.us/wdehome.html | http://www.asme.com/wycas/index.htm |

**Table 2**  Norm-Referenced and Criterion-Referenced Tests Administered by State

| STATE | NORM-REFERENCED TEST | CRITERION-REFERENCED TEST | EXIT EXAM |
|---|---|---|---|
| Alabama | Stanford Achievement Test | | Alabama High School Graduation Exam |
| Alaska | California Achievement Test | Alaska Benchmark Examinations | |
| Arizona | Stanford Achievement Test | Arizona's Instrument to Measure Standards (AIMS) | |
| Arkansas | Stanford Achievement Test | | |
| California | Stanford Achievement Test | Standardized Testing and Reporting Supplement | High School Exit Exam (HSEE) |
| Colorado | None | Colorado Student Assessment Program | |
| Connecticut | | Connecticut Mastery Test | |
| Delaware | Stanford Achievement Test | Delaware Student Testing Program | |
| District of Columbia | Stanford Achievement Test | | |
| Florida | (Locally Selected) | Florida Comprehensive Assessment Test (FCAT) | High School Competency Test (HSCT) |
| Georgia | Stanford Achievement Test | Georgia Kindergarten Assessment Program—Revised and Criterion-Referenced Competency Tests (CRCT) | Georgia High School Graduation Tests |
| Hawaii | Stanford Achievement Test | Credit by Examination | Hawaii State Test of Essential Competencies |
| Idaho | Iowa Tests of Basic Skills/ Tests of Achievement and Proficiency | Direct Writing/Mathematics Assessment, Idaho Reading Indicator | |
| Illinois | | Illinois Standards Achievement Tests | Prairie State Achievement Examination |
| Indiana | | Indiana Statewide Testing for Educational Progress | |
| Iowa | (None) | | |
| Kansas | | (State-Developed Tests) | |
| Kentucky | Comprehensive Test of Basic Skills | Kentucky Core Content Tests | |
| Louisiana | Iowa Tests of Basic Skills | Louisiana Educational Assessment Program | Graduate Exit Exam |
| Maine | | Maine Educational Assessment | High School Assessment Test |
| Maryland | | Maryland School Performance Assessment Program, Maryland Functional Testing Program | |

| STATE | NORM-REFERENCED TEST | CRITERION-REFERENCED TEST | EXIT EXAM |
|---|---|---|---|
| Massachusetts | | Massachusetts Comprehensive Assessment System | |
| Michigan | | Michigan Educational Assessment Program | High School Test |
| Minnesota | | Basic Standards Test | Profile of Learning |
| Mississippi | Comprehensive Test of Basic Skills | Subject Area Testing Program | Functional Literacy Examination |
| Missouri | | Missouri Mastery and Achievement Test | |
| Montana | Iowa Tests of Basic Skills | | |
| Nebraska | | | |
| Nevada | TerraNova | | Nevada High School Proficiency Examination |
| New Hampshire | | NH Educational Improvement and Assessment Program | |
| New Jersey | | Elementary School Proficiency Test/Early Warning Test | High School Proficiency Test |
| New Mexico | TerraNova | | New Mexico High School Competency Exam |
| New York | | Pupil Evaluation Program/ Preliminary Competency Tests | Regents Competency Tests |
| North Carolina | Iowa Tests of Basic Skills | NC End of Grade Test | |
| North Dakota | TerraNova | ND Reading, Writing, Speaking, Listening, Math Test | |
| Ohio | | Ohio Proficiency Tests | Ohio Proficiency Tests |
| Oklahoma | Iowa Tests of Basic Skills | Oklahoma Criterion- Referenced Tests | |
| Oregon | | Oregon Statewide Assessment | |
| Pennsylvania | | Pennsylvania System of School Assessment | |
| Rhode Island | Metropolitan Achievement Test | New Standards English Language Arts Reference Exam, New Standards Mathematics Reference Exam, Rhode Island Writing Assessment, and Rhode Island Health Education Assessment | |
| South Carolina | TerraNova | Palmetto Achievement Challenge Tests | High School Exit Exam |
| South Dakota | Stanford Achievement Test | | |
| Tennessee | Tennessee Comprehensive Assessment Program | Tennessee Comprehensive Assessment Program | |

| STATE | NORM-REFERENCED TEST | CRITERION-REFERENCED TEST | EXIT EXAM |
|---|---|---|---|
| Texas | | Texas Assessment of Academic Skills, End-of-Course Examinations | Texas Assessment of Academic Skills |
| Utah | Stanford Achievement Test | Core Curriculum Testing | |
| Vermont | | New Standards Reference Exams | |
| Virginia | Stanford Achievement Test | Virginia Standards of Learning | Virginia Standards of Learning |
| Washington | Iowa Tests of Basic Skills | Washington Assessment of Student Learning | Washington Assessment of Student Learning |
| West Virginia | Stanford Achievement Test | | |
| Wisconsin | TerraNova | Wisconsin Knowledge and Concepts Examinations | |
| Wyoming | TerraNova | Wyoming Comprehensive Assessment System | Wyoming Comprehensive Assessment System |

**Table 3**  Standardized Test Schedules by State

| STATE | KG | 1 | 2 | 3 | 4 | 5 | 6 | 7 | 8 | 9 | 10 | 11 | 12 | COMMENT |
|---|---|---|---|---|---|---|---|---|---|---|---|---|---|---|
| Alabama | | | | X | X | X | X | X | X | X | X | X | X | |
| Alaska | | | | X | X | | X | | X | | X | | | |
| Arizona | | | X | X | X | X | X | X | X | X | X | X | X | |
| Arkansas | | | | X | X | | X | X | | X | X | X | | |
| California | | | X | X | X | X | X | X | X | X | X | X | | |
| Colorado | | | | X | X | X | | X | X | | | | | |
| Connecticut | | | | | X | | X | | X | | | | | |
| Delaware | | | | X | X | X | | | X | | X | X | | |
| District of Columbia | | X | X | X | X | X | X | X | X | X | X | X | | |
| Florida | | | | X | X | X | | | X | | X | | | There is no state-mandated norm-referenced testing. However, the state collects information furnished by local districts that elect to perform norm-referenced testing. The FCAT is administered to Grades 4, 8, and 10 to assess reading and Grades 5, 8, and 10 to assess math. |
| Georgia | X | | | X | X | X | X | | X | | X | | | |
| Hawaii | | | | X | | | X | | X | | X | | | The Credit by Examination is voluntary and is given in Grade 8 in Algebra and Foreign Languages. |
| Idaho | | | | X | X | X | X | X | X | X | X | X | | |
| Illinois | | | | X | X | X | | X | X | | X | X | | Exit Exam failure will not disqualify students from graduation if all other requirements are met. |
| Indiana | | | | X | | | X | | X | | X | | | |
| Iowa | | * | * | * | * | * | * | * | * | * | * | * | * | *Iowa does not currently have a statewide testing program. Locally chosen assessments are administered to grades determined locally. |
| Kansas | | | | X | X | X | | X | X | | X | X | | |

| STATE | KG | 1 | 2 | 3 | 4 | 5 | 6 | 7 | 8 | 9 | 10 | 11 | 12 | COMMENT |
|---|---|---|---|---|---|---|---|---|---|---|---|---|---|---|
| Kentucky | | | | | X | X | X | X | X | X | X | X | X | |
| Louisiana | | | | X | X | X | X | X | X | X | X | X | X | |
| Maine | | | | | X | | | | X | | | X | | |
| Maryland | | | | X | | X | | | X | X | X | X | X | |
| Massachusetts | | | | X | X | X | | X | X | X | X | | | |
| Michigan | | | | | X | X | | X | X | | | | | |
| Minnesota | | | | X | | X | | | X | X | X | X | X | |
| Mississippi | | | | X | X | X | X | X | X | | | | | Mississippi officials would not return phone calls or emails regarding this information. |
| Missouri | | | X | X | X | X | X | X | X | X | X | | | |
| Montana | | | | | X | | | | X | | | X | | The State Board of Education has decided to use a single norm-referenced test statewide beginning 2000–2001 school year. |
| Nebraska | | ** | ** | ** | ** | ** | ** | ** | ** | ** | ** | ** | ** | **Decisions regarding testing are left to the individual school districts. |
| Nevada | | | | | X | | | | X | | | | | Districts choose whether and how to test with norm-referenced tests. |
| New Hampshire | | | | X | | | X | | | | X | | | |
| New Jersey | | | | X | X | | | X | X | X | X | X | | |
| New Mexico | | | | | X | | X | | X | | | | | |
| New York | | | | X | X | X | X | X | X | X | | | X | Assessment program is going through major revisions. |
| North Carolina | X | | | X | X | X | X | | X | X | | | X | NRT Testing selects samples of students, not all. |
| North Dakota | | | | | X | | X | | X | | X | | | |
| Ohio | | | | | X | | X | | | X | | | X | |
| Oklahoma | | | | X | | X | | X | X | | | X | | |
| Oregon | | | | X | | X | | | X | | X | | | |

| STATE | KG | 1 | 2 | 3 | 4 | 5 | 6 | 7 | 8 | 9 | 10 | 11 | 12 | COMMENT |
|---|---|---|---|---|---|---|---|---|---|---|---|---|---|---|
| Pennsylvania | | | | | | X | X | | X | X | | X | | |
| Rhode Island | | | | X | X | X | | X | X | X | X | X | | |
| South Carolina | | | | X | X | X | X | X | X | X | X | *** | *** | ***Students who fail the High School Exit Exam have opportunities to take the exam again in grades 11 and 12. |
| South Dakota | | | X | | X | X | | | X | X | | X | | |
| Tennessee | | | X | X | X | X | X | X | X | | | | | |
| Texas | | | | X | X | X | X | X | X | | X | X | X | |
| Utah | X | X | X | X | X | X | X | X | X | X | X | X | X | |
| Vermont | | | | | X | X | X | | X | X | X | X | | Rated by the Centers for Fair and Open Testing as a nearly model system for assessment. |
| Virginia | | | | X | X | X | X | | X | X | | X | | |
| Washington | | | | | X | | | X | | | X | | | |
| West Virginia | | | | X | X | X | X | X | X | X | X | X | | |
| Wisconsin | | | | | X | | | | X | | X | | | |
| Wyoming | | | | | X | | | | X | | | X | | |

# Testing Accommodations

The more testing procedures vary from one classroom or school to the next, the less we can compare the scores from one group to another. Consider a test in which the publisher recommends that three sections of the test be given in one 45-minute session per day on three consecutive days. School A follows those directions. To save time, School B gives all three sections of the test in one session lasting slightly more than two hours. We can't say that both schools followed the same testing procedures. Remember that the test publishers provide testing procedures so schools can administer the tests in as close a manner as possible to the way the tests were administered to the groups used to obtain test norms. When we compare students' scores to norms, we want to compare apples to apples, not apples to oranges.

Most schools justifiably resist making any changes in testing procedures. Informally, a teacher can make minor changes that don't alter the testing procedures, such as separating two students who talk with each other instead of paying attention to the test; letting Lisa, who is getting over an ear infection, sit closer to the front so she can hear better; or moving Jeffrey away from the window to prevent his looking out the window and daydreaming.

There are two groups of students who require more formal testing accommodations. One group of students is identified as having a disability under Section 504 of the Rehabilitation Act of 1973 (Public Law 93-112). These students face some challenge but, with reasonable and appropriate accommodation, can take advantage of the same educational opportunities as other students. That is, they have a condition that requires some accommodation for them.

Just as schools must remove physical barriers to accommodate students with disabilities, they must make appropriate accommodations to remove other types of barriers to students' access to education. Marie is profoundly deaf, even with strong hearing aids. She does well in school with the aid of an interpreter, who signs her teacher's instructions to her and tells her teacher what Marie says in reply. An appropriate accommodation for Marie would be to provide the interpreter to sign test instructions to her, or to allow her to watch a videotape with an interpreter signing test instructions. Such a reasonable accommodation would not deviate from standard testing procedures and, in fact, would ensure that Marie received the same instructions as the other students.

If your child is considered disabled and has what is generally called a Section 504 Plan or individual accommodation plan (IAP), then the appropriate way to ask for testing accommodations is to ask for them in a meeting to discuss school accommodations under the plan. If your child is not already covered by such a plan, he or she won't qualify for one merely because you request testing accommodations.

The other group of students who may receive formal testing accommodations are those identified as handicapped under the Individuals with Disabilities Education Act (IDEA)—students with mental retardation, learning disabilities, serious emotional disturbance, orthopedic handicap, hearing or visual problems, and other handicaps defined in the law. These students have been identified under procedures governed by federal and sometimes state law, and their education is governed by a document called the Individualized Educational Program (IEP). Unless you are under a court order specifically revoking your educational rights on behalf of your child, you are a full member of the IEP team even if you and your child's other parent are divorced and the other parent has custody. Until recently, IEP teams actually had the prerogative to exclude certain handicapped students from taking standardized group testing altogether. However, today states make it more difficult to exclude students from testing.

If your child is classified as handicapped and has an IEP, the appropriate place to ask for testing accommodations is in an IEP team meeting. In fact, federal regulations require IEP teams to address testing accommodations. You have the right to call a meeting at any time. In that meeting, you will have the opportunity to present your case for the accommodations you believe are necessary. Be prepared for the other team members to resist making extreme accommodations unless you can present a very strong case. If your child is identified as handicapped and you believe that he or she should be provided special testing accommodations, contact the person at your child's school who is responsible for convening IEP meetings and request a meeting to discuss testing accommodations.

Problems arise when a request is made for accommodations that cause major departures from standard testing procedures. For example, Lynn has an identified learning disability in mathematics calculation and attends resource classes for math. Her disability is so severe that her IEP calls for her to use a calculator when performing all math problems. She fully under-

stands math concepts, but she simply can't perform the calculations without the aid of a calculator. Now it's time for Lynn to take the school-based standardized tests, and she asks to use a calculator. In this case, since her IEP already requires her to be provided with a calculator when performing math calculations, she may be allowed a calculator during school standardized tests. However, because using a calculator constitutes a major violation of standard testing procedures, her score on all sections in which she is allowed to use a calculator will be recorded as a failure, and her results in some states will be removed from among those of other students in her school in calculating school results.

How do we determine whether a student is allowed formal accommodations in standardized school testing and what these accommodations may be? First, if your child is not already identified as either handicapped or disabled, having the child classified in either group solely to receive testing accommodations will be considered a violation of the laws governing both classifications. Second, even if your child is already classified in either group, your state's department of public instruction will provide strict guidelines for the testing accommodations schools may make. Third, even if your child is classified in either group and you are proposing testing accommodations allowed under state testing guidelines, any accommodations must still be both *reasonable* and *appropriate*. To be reasonable and appropriate, testing accommodations must relate to your child's disability and must be similar to those already in place in his or her daily educational program. If your child is always tested individually in a separate room for all tests in all subjects, then a similar practice in taking school-based standardized tests may be appropriate. But if your child has a learning disability only in mathematics calculation, requesting that all test questions be read to him or her is inappropriate because that accommodation does not relate to his identified handicap.

# Glossary

**Accountability**   The idea that a school district is held responsible for the achievement of its students. The term may also be applied to holding students responsible for a certain level of achievement in order to be promoted or to graduate.

**Achievement test**   An assessment that measures current knowledge in one or more of the areas taught in most schools, such as reading, math, and language arts.

**Aptitude test**   An assessment designed to predict a student's potential for learning knowledge or skills.

**Content validity**   The extent to which a test represents the content it is designed to cover.

**Criterion-referenced test**   A test that rates how thoroughly a student has mastered a specific skill or area of knowledge. Typically, a criterion-referenced test is subjective, and relies on someone to observe and rate student work; it doesn't allow for easy comparisons of achievement among students. Performance assessments are criterion-referenced tests. The opposite of a criterion-referenced test is a norm-referenced test.

**Frequency distribution**   A tabulation of individual scores (or groups of scores) that shows the number of persons who obtained each score.

**Generalizability**   The idea that the score on a test reflects what a child knows about a subject, or how well he performs the skills the test is supposed to be assessing. Generalizability requires that enough test items are administered to truly assess a student's achievement.

**Grade equivalent**   A score on a scale developed to indicate the school grade (usually measured in months of a year) that corresponds to an average chronological age, mental age, test score, or other characteristic. A grade equivalent of 6.4 is interpreted as a score that is average for a group in the fourth month of Grade 6.

**High-stakes assessment**   A type of standardized test that has major consequences for a student or school (such as whether a child graduates from high school or gets admitted to college).

**Mean**   Average score of a group of scores.

**Median**   The middle score in a set of scores ranked from smallest to largest.

**National percentile**   Percentile score derived from the performance of a group of individuals across the nation.

**Normative sample**   A comparison group consisting of individuals who have taken a test under standard conditions.

**Norm-referenced test**   A standardized test that can compare scores of students in one school with a reference group (usually other students in the same grade and age, called the "norm group"). Norm-referenced tests compare the achievement of one student or the students of a school, school district, or state with the norm score.

**Norms**   A summary of the performance of a group of individuals on which a test was standardized.

**Percentile**   An incorrect form of the word *centile,* which is the percent of a group of scores that falls below a given score. Although the correct term is *centile,* much of the testing literature has adopted the term *percentile.*

**Performance standards**   A level of performance on a test set by education experts.

**Quartiles**   Points that divide the frequency distribution of scores into equal fourths.

**Regression to the mean**   The tendency of scores in a group of scores to vary in the direction of the mean. For example: If a child has an abnormally low score on a test, she is likely to make a higher score (that is, one closer to the mean) the next time she takes the test.

**Reliability**   The consistency with which a test measures some trait or characteristic. A measure can be reliable without being valid, but it can't be valid without being reliable.

**Standard deviation**   A statistical measure used to describe the extent to which scores vary in a group of scores. Approximately 68 percent of scores in a group are expected to be in a range from one standard deviation below the mean to one standard deviation above the mean.

**Standardized test**   A test that contains well-defined questions of proven validity and that produces reliable scores. Such tests are commonly paper-and-pencil exams containing multiple-choice items, true or false questions, matching exercises, or short fill-in-the-blanks items. These tests may also include performance assessment items (such as a writing sample), but assessment items cannot be completed quickly or scored reliably.

**Test anxiety**   Anxiety that occurs in test-taking situations. Test anxiety can seriously impair individuals' ability to obtain accurate scores on a test.

**Validity**   The extent to which a test measures the trait or characteristic it is designed to measure. Also see *reliability.*

# Answer Keys for Practice Skills

**Chapter 2:**
**Vocabulary**

| | |
|---|---|
| 1 | A |
| 2 | D |
| 3 | D |
| 4 | B |
| 5 | B |
| 6 | D |
| 7 | B |
| 8 | B |
| 9 | D |
| 10 | B |
| 11 | D |
| 12 | A |
| 13 | A |
| 14 | A |
| 15 | C |
| 16 | B |
| 17 | A |
| 18 | D |

**Chapter 3:**
**Word Meanings**
**in Context**

| | |
|---|---|
| 1 | C |
| 2 | A |
| 3 | C |
| 4 | C |
| 5 | B |
| 6 | A |
| 7 | C |
| 8 | A |
| 9 | B |

| | |
|---|---|
| 10 | A |
| 11 | D |
| 12 | D |
| 13 | B |
| 14 | D |
| 15 | B |

**Chapter 4:**
**Antonyms,**
**Synonyms, and**
**Homophones**

| | |
|---|---|
| 1 | C |
| 2 | D |
| 3 | B |
| 4 | A |
| 5 | B |
| 6 | C |
| 7 | A |
| 8 | C |
| 9 | D |
| 10 | C |
| 11 | A |
| 12 | D |
| 13 | A |
| 14 | D |
| 15 | C |
| 16 | D |
| 17 | C |
| 18 | C |
| 19 | A |
| 20 | B |
| 21 | D |
| 22 | C |

| | |
|---|---|
| 23 | B |
| 24 | A |
| 25 | B |
| 26 | B |
| 27 | C |

**Chapter 5:**
**Word Sounds**

| | |
|---|---|
| 1 | C |
| 2 | A |
| 3 | C |
| 4 | B |
| 5 | A |
| 6 | C |
| 7 | B |
| 8 | D |
| 9 | A |
| 10 | D |
| 11 | D |
| 12 | A |
| 13 | D |
| 14 | C |
| 15 | D |
| 16 | A |
| 17 | B |
| 18 | B |
| 19 | C |
| 20 | D |

**Chapter 6:**
**Spelling**

| | |
|---|---|
| 1 | B |
| 2 | D |

| | |
|---|---|
| 3 | A |
| 4 | B |
| 5 | D |
| 6 | A |
| 7 | B |
| 8 | A |
| 9 | B |
| 10 | D |
| 11 | A |
| 12 | B |
| 13 | C |
| 14 | A |
| 15 | B |
| 16 | A |
| 17 | C |
| 18 | B |
| 19 | C |
| 20 | D |
| 21 | B |
| 22 | A |
| 23 | C |
| 24 | A |
| 25 | C |

**Chapter 7:**
**Capitalization and**
**Punctuation**

| | |
|---|---|
| 1 | B |
| 2 | D |
| 3 | D |
| 4 | A |
| 5 | B |
| 6 | D |

| | |
|---|---|
| 7 | B |
| 8 | A |
| 9 | A |
| 10 | B |
| 11 | A |
| 12 | D |
| 13 | B |

## Chapter 8:
## Grammar Rules

| | |
|---|---|
| 1 | D |
| 2 | B |
| 3 | B |
| 4 | A |
| 5 | B |
| 6 | C |
| 7 | D |
| 8 | A |
| 9 | B |
| 10 | D |
| 11 | B |
| 12 | B |

## Chapter 9:
## Breaking It Down

| | |
|---|---|
| 1 | B |
| 2 | C |
| 3 | D |
| 4 | A |
| 5 | C |
| 6 | D |
| 7 | B |
| 8 | B |
| 9 | B |
| 10 | D |
| 11 | C |
| 12 | D |
| 13 | B |
| 14 | B |
| 15 | B |

## Chapter 10:
## Reading
## Comprehension

| | |
|---|---|
| 1 | B |
| 2 | C |

| | |
|---|---|
| 3 | A |
| 4 | A |
| 5 | A |
| 6 | B |
| 7 | B |
| 8 | D |
| 9 | C |
| 10 | C |

## Chapter 11:
## Literary Genres

| | |
|---|---|
| 1 | D |
| 2 | C |
| 3 | B |
| 4 | A |
| 5 | B |
| 6 | B |
| 7 | D |
| 8 | C |
| 9 | B |
| 10 | B |
| 11 | B |
| 12 | C |

| | |
|---|---|
| 13 | B |
| 14 | D |

## Chapter 12:
## Study Skills

| | |
|---|---|
| 1 | B |
| 2 | C |
| 3 | A |
| 4 | A |
| 5 | B |
| 6 | D |
| 7 | C |
| 8 | D |
| 9 | B |
| 10 | A |
| 11 | A |
| 12 | D |
| 13 | C |
| 14 | A |

# Sample Practice Test

You may be riding a roller coaster of feelings and opinions at this point. If your child has gone through the preceding chapters easily, then you're both probably excited to move on, to jump in with both feet, take the test, and that will be that. On the other hand, your child may have struggled a bit as he worked through some of the chapters. Some of the concepts may be difficult to understand, and some of the skills will require a little more practice. Never fear! All children acquire skills in areas of learning only when they are developmentally ready.

We can't push children beyond their own individual internal limits, but we can reinforce the skills that they are already in the process of developing. In addition, we can play games and engage in other activities to pave the way for their understanding of the skills and concepts that lie ahead. With luck, that's what you've done with the preceding chapters.

The test that follows is designed using components of several different kinds of standardized tests. The test that your child takes in school probably won't look just like this one, but it will be close enough that when he takes a "real" test, he should be pretty comfortable with the format. The administration of tests varies as well. It is important that your child hear the rhythm and language used in standardized tests. If you wish, you may have your child read the directions that precede each test section to you first and explain what the item is asking him to do. Your child may then proceed on his own if you feel he understands it, or you may want to clarify the instructions.

## Test Administration

If you like, your child may complete the entire test in one day, but it is not recommended that your child attempt to finish it in one sitting. Instead, take breaks frequently. As test administrator, you'll find that you'll need to stretch, have a snack, or use the bathroom too! If you plan to do the test in one day, leave at least 15 minutes between sessions.

Before you start, prepare a quiet place, free of distractions. Have on hand two or three sharpened pencils with erasers that don't smudge and a flat, clear work space. As your child proceeds from item to item, encourage him to ask you questions if he doesn't understand something. In a real testing situation, questions are accepted, but the extent to which items can be explained is limited. Don't go overboard in making sure your child understands what to do. He'll have to learn to trust his instincts somewhat.

The test shouldn't take all day. If your youngster seems to be dawdling along, set and enforce time limits, and help him to understand that the real test will have time limits as well. Finally, relax, and try to have fun!

## To the Student:

These tests will give you a chance to put the tips you have learned to work.
 A few last reminders . . .

- Be sure you understand all the directions before you begin each test. You may ask the teacher questions about the directions if you do not understand them.

- Work as quickly as you can during each test.

- When you change an answer, be sure to erase your first mark completely.

- You can guess at an answer or skip difficult items and go back to them later.

- Use the tips you have learned whenever you can.

- It is OK to be a little nervous. You may even do better.

 Now that you have completed the lessons in this book, you are on your way to scoring high!

Cut along dashed line.

| STUDENT'S NAME | SCHOOL |
| --- | --- |

LAST  FIRST  MI

TEACHER

FEMALE ◯   MALE ◯

BIRTHDATE

| MONTH | DAY | YEAR |
| --- | --- | --- |

JAN ◯
FEB ◯
MAR ◯
APR ◯
MAY ◯
JUN ◯
JUL ◯
AUG ◯
SEP ◯
OCT ◯
NOV ◯
DEC ◯

GRADE
① ② ③ ④ ⑤ ⑥

## Vocabulary

1 Ⓐ Ⓑ Ⓒ Ⓓ    2 Ⓐ Ⓑ Ⓒ Ⓓ    3 Ⓐ Ⓑ Ⓒ Ⓓ    4 Ⓐ Ⓑ Ⓒ Ⓓ    5 Ⓐ Ⓑ Ⓒ Ⓓ    6 Ⓐ Ⓑ Ⓒ Ⓓ

## Word Meanings in Context

7 Ⓐ Ⓑ Ⓒ Ⓓ    9 Ⓐ Ⓑ Ⓒ Ⓓ    11 Ⓐ Ⓑ Ⓒ Ⓓ    13 Ⓐ Ⓑ Ⓒ Ⓓ    14 Ⓐ Ⓑ Ⓒ Ⓓ    15 Ⓐ Ⓑ Ⓒ Ⓓ
8 Ⓐ Ⓑ Ⓒ Ⓓ    10 Ⓐ Ⓑ Ⓒ Ⓓ    12 Ⓐ Ⓑ Ⓒ Ⓓ

## Antonyms, Synonyms, and Homophones

16 Ⓐ Ⓑ Ⓒ Ⓓ    22 Ⓐ Ⓑ Ⓒ Ⓓ    28 Ⓐ Ⓑ Ⓒ Ⓓ    34 Ⓐ Ⓑ Ⓒ Ⓓ    40 Ⓐ Ⓑ Ⓒ Ⓓ    46 Ⓐ Ⓑ Ⓒ Ⓓ
17 Ⓐ Ⓑ Ⓒ Ⓓ    23 Ⓐ Ⓑ Ⓒ Ⓓ    29 Ⓐ Ⓑ Ⓒ Ⓓ    35 Ⓐ Ⓑ Ⓒ Ⓓ    41 Ⓐ Ⓑ Ⓒ Ⓓ    47 Ⓐ Ⓑ Ⓒ Ⓓ
18 Ⓐ Ⓑ Ⓒ Ⓓ    24 Ⓐ Ⓑ Ⓒ Ⓓ    30 Ⓐ Ⓑ Ⓒ Ⓓ    36 Ⓐ Ⓑ Ⓒ Ⓓ    42 Ⓐ Ⓑ Ⓒ Ⓓ    48 Ⓐ Ⓑ Ⓒ Ⓓ
19 Ⓐ Ⓑ Ⓒ Ⓓ    25 Ⓐ Ⓑ Ⓒ Ⓓ    31 Ⓐ Ⓑ Ⓒ Ⓓ    37 Ⓐ Ⓑ Ⓒ Ⓓ    43 Ⓐ Ⓑ Ⓒ Ⓓ    49 Ⓐ Ⓑ Ⓒ Ⓓ
20 Ⓐ Ⓑ Ⓒ Ⓓ    26 Ⓐ Ⓑ Ⓒ Ⓓ    32 Ⓐ Ⓑ Ⓒ Ⓓ    38 Ⓐ Ⓑ Ⓒ Ⓓ    44 Ⓐ Ⓑ Ⓒ Ⓓ    50 Ⓐ Ⓑ Ⓒ Ⓓ
21 Ⓐ Ⓑ Ⓒ Ⓓ    27 Ⓐ Ⓑ Ⓒ Ⓓ    33 Ⓐ Ⓑ Ⓒ Ⓓ    39 Ⓐ Ⓑ Ⓒ Ⓓ    45 Ⓐ Ⓑ Ⓒ Ⓓ    51 Ⓐ Ⓑ Ⓒ Ⓓ

## Word Sounds

52 Ⓐ Ⓑ Ⓒ Ⓓ    56 Ⓐ Ⓑ Ⓒ Ⓓ    60 Ⓐ Ⓑ Ⓒ Ⓓ    63 Ⓐ Ⓑ Ⓒ Ⓓ    66 Ⓐ Ⓑ Ⓒ Ⓓ    69 Ⓐ Ⓑ Ⓒ Ⓓ
53 Ⓐ Ⓑ Ⓒ Ⓓ    57 Ⓐ Ⓑ Ⓒ Ⓓ    61 Ⓐ Ⓑ Ⓒ Ⓓ    64 Ⓐ Ⓑ Ⓒ Ⓓ    67 Ⓐ Ⓑ Ⓒ Ⓓ    70 Ⓐ Ⓑ Ⓒ Ⓓ
54 Ⓐ Ⓑ Ⓒ Ⓓ    58 Ⓐ Ⓑ Ⓒ Ⓓ    62 Ⓐ Ⓑ Ⓒ Ⓓ    65 Ⓐ Ⓑ Ⓒ Ⓓ    68 Ⓐ Ⓑ Ⓒ Ⓓ    71 Ⓐ Ⓑ Ⓒ Ⓓ
55 Ⓐ Ⓑ Ⓒ Ⓓ    59 Ⓐ Ⓑ Ⓒ Ⓓ

## Spelling

72 Ⓐ Ⓑ Ⓒ Ⓓ    76 Ⓐ Ⓑ Ⓒ Ⓓ    80 Ⓐ Ⓑ Ⓒ Ⓓ    84 Ⓐ Ⓑ Ⓒ Ⓓ    88 Ⓐ Ⓑ Ⓒ Ⓓ    92 Ⓐ Ⓑ Ⓒ Ⓓ
73 Ⓐ Ⓑ Ⓒ Ⓓ    77 Ⓐ Ⓑ Ⓒ Ⓓ    81 Ⓐ Ⓑ Ⓒ Ⓓ    85 Ⓐ Ⓑ Ⓒ Ⓓ    89 Ⓐ Ⓑ Ⓒ Ⓓ    93 Ⓐ Ⓑ Ⓒ Ⓓ
74 Ⓐ Ⓑ Ⓒ Ⓓ    78 Ⓐ Ⓑ Ⓒ Ⓓ    82 Ⓐ Ⓑ Ⓒ Ⓓ    86 Ⓐ Ⓑ Ⓒ Ⓓ    90 Ⓐ Ⓑ Ⓒ Ⓓ    94 Ⓐ Ⓑ Ⓒ Ⓓ
75 Ⓐ Ⓑ Ⓒ Ⓓ    79 Ⓐ Ⓑ Ⓒ Ⓓ    83 Ⓐ Ⓑ Ⓒ Ⓓ    87 Ⓐ Ⓑ Ⓒ Ⓓ    91 Ⓐ Ⓑ Ⓒ Ⓓ    95 Ⓐ Ⓑ Ⓒ Ⓓ

## Capitalization and Punctuation

96 Ⓐ Ⓑ Ⓒ Ⓓ    98 Ⓐ Ⓑ Ⓒ Ⓓ    100 Ⓐ Ⓑ Ⓒ Ⓓ    102 Ⓐ Ⓑ Ⓒ Ⓓ    104 Ⓐ Ⓑ Ⓒ Ⓓ    106 Ⓐ Ⓑ Ⓒ Ⓓ
97 Ⓐ Ⓑ Ⓒ Ⓓ    99 Ⓐ Ⓑ Ⓒ Ⓓ    101 Ⓐ Ⓑ Ⓒ Ⓓ    103 Ⓐ Ⓑ Ⓒ Ⓓ    105 Ⓐ Ⓑ Ⓒ Ⓓ    107 Ⓐ Ⓑ Ⓒ Ⓓ

## Grammar Rules

108 Ⓐ Ⓑ Ⓒ Ⓓ    111 Ⓐ Ⓑ Ⓒ Ⓓ    114 Ⓐ Ⓑ Ⓒ Ⓓ    117 Ⓐ Ⓑ Ⓒ Ⓓ    120 Ⓐ Ⓑ Ⓒ Ⓓ    123 Ⓐ Ⓑ Ⓒ Ⓓ
109 Ⓐ Ⓑ Ⓒ Ⓓ    112 Ⓐ Ⓑ Ⓒ Ⓓ    115 Ⓐ Ⓑ Ⓒ Ⓓ    118 Ⓐ Ⓑ Ⓒ Ⓓ    121 Ⓐ Ⓑ Ⓒ Ⓓ    124 Ⓐ Ⓑ Ⓒ Ⓓ
110 Ⓐ Ⓑ Ⓒ Ⓓ    113 Ⓐ Ⓑ Ⓒ Ⓓ    116 Ⓐ Ⓑ Ⓒ Ⓓ    119 Ⓐ Ⓑ Ⓒ Ⓓ    122 Ⓐ Ⓑ Ⓒ Ⓓ    125 Ⓐ Ⓑ Ⓒ Ⓓ

## Reading Comprehension

126 Ⓐ Ⓑ Ⓒ Ⓓ    130 Ⓐ Ⓑ Ⓒ Ⓓ    134 Ⓐ Ⓑ Ⓒ Ⓓ    137 Ⓐ Ⓑ Ⓒ Ⓓ    140 Ⓐ Ⓑ Ⓒ Ⓓ    143 Ⓐ Ⓑ Ⓒ Ⓓ
127 Ⓐ Ⓑ Ⓒ Ⓓ    131 Ⓐ Ⓑ Ⓒ Ⓓ    135 Ⓐ Ⓑ Ⓒ Ⓓ    138 Ⓐ Ⓑ Ⓒ Ⓓ    141 Ⓐ Ⓑ Ⓒ Ⓓ    144 Ⓐ Ⓑ Ⓒ Ⓓ
128 Ⓐ Ⓑ Ⓒ Ⓓ    132 Ⓐ Ⓑ Ⓒ Ⓓ    136 Ⓐ Ⓑ Ⓒ Ⓓ    139 Ⓐ Ⓑ Ⓒ Ⓓ    142 Ⓐ Ⓑ Ⓒ Ⓓ    145 Ⓐ Ⓑ Ⓒ Ⓓ
129 Ⓐ Ⓑ Ⓒ Ⓓ    133 Ⓐ Ⓑ Ⓒ Ⓓ

Cut along dashed line.

## Literary Genres

146 (A) (B) (C) (D)   148 (A) (B) (C) (D)   150 (A) (B) (C) (D)   152 (A) (B) (C) (D)   154 (A) (B) (C) (D)   155 (A) (B) (C) (D)

147 (A) (B) (C) (D)   149 (A) (B) (C) (D)   151 (A) (B) (C) (D)   153 (A) (B) (C) (D)

## Study Skills

156 (A) (B) (C) (D)   158 (A) (B) (C) (D)   159 (A) (B) (C) (D)   160 (A) (B) (C) (D)   161 (A) (B) (C) (D)   162 (A) (B) (C) (D)

157 (A) (B) (C) (D)

# VOCABULARY

Cut along dashed line.

**Directions:** Choose the correct word to go in the blank in these sentences.

**Example:**

The rabbit popped down into his _____.

**A** bed

**B** bone

**C** hole

**D** grass

**Answer:**

**C** hole

1 If I make a mistake on the test, I can use a(n) _____.

**A** pencil

**B** pen

**C** ruler

**D** eraser

2 Will you help me _____ the necklace that I lost?

**A** find

**B** lose

**C** see

**D** hear

3 As the sun rose, we heard a _____ crow.

**A** pig

**B** rooster

**C** cow

**D** owl

4 Jim was _____ because his new business venture was a success.

**A** angry

**B** sad

**C** jealous

**D** happy

**Directions:** Choose the answer that means the same as the underlined word.

**Example:** Tom lost a <u>pair</u> of bookends.

**A** group

**B** set of two

**C** bunch

**D** single

**Answer:**

**B** set of two

123

**5** If the path is <u>faint</u> it is

  **A** twisted.

  **B** crooked.

  **C** dark.

  **D** unclear.

**6** A <u>colt</u> is a

  **A** kind of dress.

  **B** baby deer.

  **C** baby horse.

  **D** type of cereal.

STOP

Cut along dashed line.

# WORD MEANINGS IN CONTEXT

**Directions:** Choose the sentence below in which the underlined word means the same thing as it means in the question.

**Example:**

Suzy can't <u>bear</u> to watch sad movies.

**A** Jed can't <u>bear</u> to tell the queen the bad news.

**B** The big black <u>bear</u> came lumbering out of the woods.

**C** I don't think you should <u>bear</u> a grudge.

**D** The soldier had the right to <u>bear</u> arms.

**Answer:**

**A** Jed can't <u>bear</u> to tell the queen the bad news.

---

**7** Kara likes to smell the fresh <u>air</u>.

**A** Brittany played a Scottish <u>air</u> on the piano.

**B** This fish could not breathe in the <u>air</u>.

**C** The lonely man shed a tear when he heard the sad news <u>air</u> on the radio.

**D** Miranda's mother will <u>air</u> out the sheets.

---

**8** She was wearing a diamond <u>ring</u>.

**A** I did not hear the phone <u>ring</u>.

**B** Sally drew a <u>ring</u> in the sand.

**C** Don't you like this ruby <u>ring</u>?

**D** There is a <u>ring</u> around the collar.

---

**Directions:** For the following questions, choose the answer that means the same as the underlined word.

**Example:**

The boy seldom looked before he <u>leaped</u>.

**A** ran

**B** jumped

**C** parked

**D** swam

**Answer:**

**B** jumped

---

**9** John was <u>glad</u> to finish the game.

**A** unhappy

**B** excited

**C** slow

**D** quick

---

125

**10** Jody was <u>angry</u> at her best friend for cheating.

   **A** unhappy

   **B** mad

   **C** giggly

   **D** content

**11** The pitcher <u>tossed</u> the ball to the batter.

   **A** threw away

   **B** kept

   **C** caught

   **D** threw

**12** Sam <u>occasionally</u> forgets his homework.

   **A** rarely

   **B** usually

   **C** once in a while

   **D** never

**13** The dog <u>growled</u> with menace.

   **A** shouted

   **B** sobbed

   **C** snarled

   **D** grinned

**14** The tree fell over with a <u>noisy</u> crack!

   **A** very

   **B** silent

   **C** loud

   **D** dark

**15** The cow <u>ran</u> into the barn.

   **A** sauntered

   **B** walked

   **C** galloped

   **D** mooed

Cut along dashed line.

STOP

# ANTONYMS, SYNONYMS, AND HOMOPHONES

**Directions:** Choose the pair of synonyms from the word pairs listed below.

**Example:**

| | | |
|---|---|---|
| **A** | run | walk |
| **B** | spin | turn |
| **C** | fly | flea |
| **D** | see | sea |

**Answer:**

| | | |
|---|---|---|
| **B** | spin | turn |

| | | | |
|---|---|---|---|
| **16** | **A** | is | was |
| | **B** | halt | stop |
| | **C** | ugly | pretty |
| | **D** | green | blue |

| | | | |
|---|---|---|---|
| **17** | **A** | who's | whose |
| | **B** | read | write |
| | **C** | pretty | beautiful |
| | **D** | rush | stop |

| | | | |
|---|---|---|---|
| **18** | **A** | buy | purchase |
| | **B** | bed | chair |
| | **C** | sink | float |
| | **D** | flee | flea |

**Directions:** Choose the pair of words from the list below that is **not** a pair of synonyms.

**Example:**

| | | |
|---|---|---|
| **A** | run | walk |
| **B** | spin | turn |
| **C** | fly | soar |
| **D** | see | spy |

**Answer:**

| | | |
|---|---|---|
| **A** | run | walk |

| | | | |
|---|---|---|---|
| **19** | **A** | baby | infant |
| | **B** | tired | sleepy |
| | **C** | bad | good |
| | **D** | cheerful | pleasant |

| | | | |
|---|---|---|---|
| **20** | **A** | eyes | ears |
| | **B** | book | volume |
| | **C** | nice | kind |
| | **D** | big | little |

| | | | |
|---|---|---|---|
| **21** | **A** | seldom | rarely |
| | **B** | pretty | lovely |
| | **C** | loud | soft |
| | **D** | skip | hop |

GO

**Directions:** Read each sentence below and choose the word that is an antonym of the underlined word in the sentence.

**Example:**

Emma was <u>angry</u> about losing the game.

A furious

B happy

C hungry

D sad

**Answer:**

B happy

---

22 The dress was very <u>short</u>.

A long

B ugly

C beautiful

D green

---

23 John was a <u>powerful</u> king.

A bad

B smart

C strong

D weak

---

24 Gallileo was a <u>brilliant</u> astronomer.

A unintelligent

B smart

C funny

D angry

---

25 Rachel <u>loved</u> to ride horses.

A tricky

B dumb

C sly

D hated

---

**Directions:** Read each sentence below. Choose the word that means the opposite of the underlined word in the sentence.

**Example:**

at the <u>front</u> of the class

A rear

B middle

C side

D back

**Answer:**

D back

Cut along dashed line.

GO

Cut along dashed line.

**26** We must <u>start</u> the game.

    **A** play

    **B** continue

    **C** hear

    **D** end

**27** Let's go <u>forward</u>.

    **A** backward

    **B** inside

    **C** outside

    **D** upside down

**28** Julie is going to come home <u>late</u>.

    **A** tonight

    **B** eventually

    **C** early

    **D** other

**29** I'm having trouble <u>pushing</u> the cart up the hill.

    **A** crying

    **B** running

    **C** pulling

    **D** starting

**30** Have you <u>finished</u> the project?

    **A** started

    **B** ended

    **C** stopped

    **D** abandoned

**Directions:** Choose the pair of antonyms in the choices below.

**Example:**

    **A** yes      no

    **B** high      lofty

    **C** tired      sleepy

    **D** burn      sizzle

**Answer:**

    **A** yes      no

**31**   **A** straight      up

    **B** right      wrong

    **C** started      begin

    **D** sing      sleep

**32**   **A** old      ancient

    **B** thin      skinny

    **C** curly      frizzy

    **D** fast      slow

GO

**33**  **A**  spin          twirl

   **B**  car            auto

   **C**  push           pull

   **D**  cold           icy

**34**  **A**  smile          grin

   **B**  race           run

   **C**  sturdy         strong

   **D**  black          white

**35**  **A**  wet            soaked

   **B**  cold           freezing

   **C**  dark           light

   **D**  fur            fir

**36**  **A**  heavy          large

   **B**  sink           sink

   **C**  sweet          sour

   **D**  cry            sob

**Directions:** Choose the pair of words from the list below that is **not** a pair of antonyms.

**Example:**

   **A**  run            walk

   **B**  loud           noisy

   **C**  fly            fall

   **D**  see            hide

**Answer:**

   **B**  loud           noisy

**37**  **A**  hear           listen

   **B**  remember       forget

   **C**  polite         rude

   **D**  mean           nice

**38**  **A**  hungry         full

   **B**  break          shatter

   **C**  skinny         fat

   **D**  buy            sell

**39**  **A**  quiet          loud

   **B**  salt           pepper

   **C**  drink          eat

   **D**  chorus         choir

**Directions:** Read each passage. For each blank, choose the word that best fits in the sentence.

**Example:**

It was time to go to the party. Susie ran out the ___ carrying a _____.

   **A**  bed            **A**  bike

   **B**  door           **B**  cake

   **C**  window         **C**  bucket

   **D**  bun            **D**  bus

**Answer:**

    **B** door       **B** cake

Firefighters wear clothes made of special __40__ to protect themselves from __41__, flames, and smoke. They use gloves and hats that won't __42__.

**40 A** fur

    **B** material

    **C** buttons

    **D** cement

**41 A** air

    **B** lightning

    **C** cold

    **D** heat

**42 A** wear out

    **B** rust

    **C** freeze

    **D** burn

String instruments work when someone touches the strings to make them __43__. To play a violin, you need a __44__. Guitars are string instruments, too.

**43 A** howl       **B** vibrate

    **C** freeze    **D** shiver

**44 A** suit

    **B** hat

    **C** bow

    **D** harp

For thousands of years the people of the Middle East have wrapped __45__ around their heads to protect them from the wind and the hot desert __46__. They ride camels who can survive without drinking a lot; they walk long distances without __47__.

**45 A** trinkets

    **B** hats

    **C** cloth

    **D** ice cubes

**46 A** water

    **B** fires

    **C** sun

    **D** moon

**47 A** a bath

    **B** water

    **C** getting lost

    **D** slowing down

GO →

**Directions:** Read each sentence. Choose the correct word to fill in the blank.

**Example:**

Mary won a blue _____ in the horse show.

**A** purse     **B** tourniquet

**C** ribbon     **D** book

**Answer:**

**C** ribbon

---

**48** Karen and Jim stared in _____ at the beautiful work of art.

**A** horror     **B** wonder

**C** coolness     **D** tiredness

---

**49** Bob will have to save his allowance since the price of the football is so much _____ than he had thought.

**A** lower     **B** higher

**C** lose     **D** increase

---

**50** The delicate breeze _____ through the trees.

**A** roared     **B** gusted

**C** blasted     **D** whispered

---

**51** The two girls enjoyed the comedy so much they thought they would never stop _____.

**A** laughing     **B** giggles

**C** crying     **D** shouting

---

STOP

# WORD SOUNDS

**Directions:** Which pair of words **begins** with the same sound?

**Example:**

| | | |
|---|---|---|
| **A** | ball | fall |
| **B** | lank | hank |
| **C** | car | kind |
| **D** | gotten | gyp |

**Answer:**

| | | |
|---|---|---|
| **C** | car | kind |

| 52 | **A** | church | chill |
|---|---|---|---|
| | **B** | think | toad |
| | **C** | catsup | money |
| | **D** | jelly | gobs |

| 53 | **A** | Jimmy | jangle |
|---|---|---|---|
| | **B** | crutch | chug |
| | **C** | green | giant |
| | **D** | kale | church |

| 54 | **A** | ballet | dungeon |
|---|---|---|---|
| | **B** | circuit | cardboard |
| | **C** | shoot | shimmy |
| | **D** | chink | canter |

**Directions:** Choose the word with the same beginning sound as the underlined word.

**Example:**

Choose the word with the same beginning sound as <u>clock</u>.

**A** creep

**B** king

**C** queen

**D** climb

**Answer:**

**D** climb

55 Choose the word that has the same **beginning** sound as <u>brat</u>.

**A** beat

**B** bridle

**C** balderdash

**D** bicycle

56 Choose the word with the same **beginning** sound as <u>kitchen</u>.

**A** Camelot

**B** chime

**C** chat

**D** got

Cut along dashed line.

**Directions:** Choose the word with the same **ending** sound as the underlined word.

**Example:**

Which of these words has the same **ending** sound as the word heath?

**A** zeal

**B** bear

**C** seat

**D** health

**Answer:**

**D** health

---

**57** Which of these words has the same **ending** sound as peach?

**A** print

**B** preach

**C** peak

**D** think

---

**58** Which of these words has the same **ending** sound as teach?

**A** teak

**B** tart

**C** reach

**D** tight

---

**59** Which of these words has the same **ending** sound as brass?

**A** compass

**B** bat

**C** scratch

**D** peek

---

**60** Which of these words has the same **ending** sound as seat?

**A** sear

**B** steer

**C** appease

**D** peat

---

**Directions:** Choose the letter blend that makes the beginning sound for each word below.

**Example:**

try

**A** T

**B** TR

**C** TRE

**D** TCH

**Answer:**

**B** TR

---

GO

Cut along dashed line.

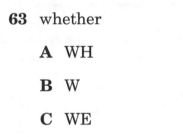

**61** shaggy

  **A** CH

  **B** S

  **C** SP

  **D** SH

**62** slimy

  **A** S

  **B** SP

  **C** ST

  **D** SL

**63** whether

  **A** WH

  **B** W

  **C** WE

  **D** H

**64** growing

  **A** G

  **B** R

  **C** GE

  **D** GR

**Directions:** Choose the letters that make the ending sound for each word below.

**Example:**

  limp

  **A** MP

  **B** NP

  **C** P

  **D** ST

**Answer:**

  **A** MP

**65** fast

  **A** T

  **B** SP

  **C** ST

  **D** SL

**66** risk

  **A** CH

  **B** CK

  **C** K

  **D** SK

**67** prettiest

  **A** ST

  **B** S

  **C** T

  **D** SH

GO

Cut along dashed line.

**Directions:** Match the word with the same vowel sound as the underlined word in each question.

**Example:**

Which word has the same **vowel** sound as in <u>roast</u>?

**A** book

**B** abode

**C** snap

**D** hop

**Answer:**

**B** abode

---

**68** What word has the same vowel sound as <u>hat</u>?

**A** hip

**B** have

**C** heard

**D** hit

---

**69** What word has the same vowel sound as <u>bright</u>?

**A** start

**B** right

**C** foal

**D** family

---

**70** What word has the same vowel sound as <u>cook</u>?

**A** wrought

**B** bright

**C** brook

**D** make

---

**71** What word has the same vowel sound as <u>cream</u>?

**A** taught

**B** bright

**C** math

**D** feet

Cut along dashed line.

STOP

# SPELLING

Cut along dashed line.

**Directions:** Choose the correctly spelled word to go into the blank.

**Example:**

Billy finished _____ of his vegetables.

**A** sum

**B** sume

**C** som

**D** some

**Answer:**

**D** some

---

**72** I could barely fit the clothes into the ____.

**A** closset

**B** closet

**C** clozet

**D** closest

---

**73** ____ was home today.

**A** nobodey

**B** nobodie

**C** noboody

**D** nobody

---

**74** The party was a _____.

**A** surprize

**B** surprise

**C** surprice

**D** surpriese

---

**75** Jim was _____ before the test.

**A** nervus

**B** nervis

**C** nervous

**D** nervouse

---

**Directions:** Pick out the word that is spelled **incorrectly** in the sentences below.

**Example:**

The principle is the head of the school district.

**A** principle

**B** head

**C** school

**D** district

**Answer:**

**A** principle

---

**76** Sudenly, the freak wind storm stopped blowing.

   **A** Sudenly

   **B** freak

   **C** storm

   **D** blowing

**77** The special event was a huge sucess.

   **A** special

   **B** event

   **C** huge

   **D** sucess

**Directions:** What is the root word in the following underlined words?

**Example:**

   nicer

   **A** nicer

   **B** nice

   **C** nices

   **D** nicest

**Answer:**

   **B** nice

**78** quickly

   **A** quick

   **B** ly

   **C** quic

   **D** kly

**79** prettiest

   **A** pretti

   **B** prettie

   **C** iest

   **D** pretty

**80** happier

   **A** happi

   **B** happie

   **C** happy

   **D** happier

**81** tresses

   **A** tress

   **B** tresse

   **C** tres

   **D** tresses

Cut along dashed line.

GO

**82** <u>making</u>

   **A** makin

   **B** make

   **C** mak

   **D** maki

**Directions:** Identify the **suffix** in each of the following words.

**Example:**

   billowing

   **A** billow

   **B** billowin

   **C** ing

   **D** all

**Answer:**

   **C** ing

**83** running

   **A** run

   **B** ng

   **C** ing

   **D** running

**84** friendless

   **A** less

   **B** le

   **C** friend

   **D** les

**85** heaving

   **A** heave

   **B** ing

   **C** eing

   **D** ving

**86** What suffix do we add to the word <u>teach</u> to make the word mean "one who teaches"?

   **A** er

   **B** or

   **C** ette

   **D** ed

Cut along dashed line.

GO

**Directions:** Identify the **prefix** in each of the following underlined words.

**Example:**

tricycle

**A** cycle

**B** tricycle

**C** tri

**D** cle

**Answer:**

**C** tri

**87** disappointed

**A** ed

**B** di

**C** dis

**D** disappoint

**88** untrue

**A** true

**B** un

**C** unt

**D** untrue

**89** retried

**A** tried

**B** ed

**C** re

**D** retry

**90** What does the prefix *re* mean in the word remake?

**A** to make down

**B** not to make

**C** to make before

**D** to make again

**91** What does the prefix *un* mean in the word unmovable?

**A** push

**B** can't be moved

**C** moved to a different place

**D** throw away

**Directions:** Choose the word that is made up of two words in the following questions.

**Example:**

**A** baseball

**B** scare

**C** falcon

**D** tighten

**Answer:**

**A** baseball

GO

**92**　**A** doghouse

　　**B** happiness

　　**C** foolish

　　**D** running

**93**　**A** skied

　　**B** skated

　　**C** backyard

　　**D** filter

**94**　**A** housing

　　**B** jumping

　　**C** hiding

　　**D** storeroom

**95**　**A** wonderful

　　**B** window

　　**C** teacup

　　**D** silliness

# CAPITALIZATION AND PUNCTUATION

**Directions:** Read these sentences. Choose the word that should begin with a capital letter.

**Example:**

We are going to new york for the holidays.

**A** are     **B** going

**C** new york     **D** holidays

**Answer:**

**C** new york

---

**96** did you see the animals in the museum?

**A** did

**B** you

**C** animals

**D** museum

---

**97** John wrote a letter to mr. Harry Truman.

**A** wrote

**B** letter

**C** to

**D** mr.

---

**98** Turning around, Paul screamed, "Hey! look out!"

**A** around

**B** screamed

**C** look

**D** out

---

**99** dear Mary: I would like you to attend my birthday party.

**A** dear

**B** would

**C** attend

**D** birthday

---

**100** On the fifth of april, we will graduate from college.

**A** fifth

**B** april

**C** graduate

**D** college

---

GO →

**Directions:** Choose the sentence that shows correct capitalization.

**Example:**

    **A** Tom and Cindy are Going to town today.

    **B** Are you going to make a Pineapple cake?

    **C** On Tuesday, we will both go to Paris.

    **D** where are you?

**Answer:**

    **C** On Tuesday, we will both go to Paris.

**101**  **A** In the Spring, Sally likes to go bike riding.

    **B** I don't like ginger Snaps.

    **C** Sam is going to school in Northern new york.

    **D** *The Grinch* is my favorite movie.

**102**  **A** My favorite dog is a Yellow lab.

    **B** Will you come to visit me at my new school in Connecticut?

    **C** At Midnight, the Halloween pranks begin!

    **D** We like to eat Beef Stew.

**103**  **A** "Look out!" She cried.

    **B** "Look Out!" She cried.

    **C** "are you going to bed yet?" She asked.

    **D** I live at 314 Tarrytown Road.

**Directions:** Choose the sentence that shows correct punctuation.

**Example:**

    **A** Sarah, come right here?

    **B** Look out!

    **C** How old are you.

    **D** Sarah ran down the hill

**Answer:**

    **B** Look out!

**104**  **A** I need to buy apples bacon and orange juice.

    **B** Hi!" she, cried happily.

    **C** "Let's go for a swim," she said.

    **D** What, shall we do today!

**105**  **A** Do you want to come with me, to the seashore?

    **B** Today is October 15 2001.

    **C** Yesterday was October, 14 2001.

    **D** Carlos did not stay to watch the baseball game; did you?

GO

Cut along dashed line.

**106**  **A**  Where are you going.

   **B**  What kind, of pie are you eating.

   **C**  "I knew that was too good to be true," he said sadly.

   **D**  "I don't know" she said quietly.

**107**  **A**  Bill Larry and Sue are going to school together.

   **B**  Will you hurry up!

   **C**  Are you going to the school play.

   **D**  Joe please take this to the teacher.

STOP

Cut along dashed line.

# GRAMMAR RULES

**Directions:** Read the following sentences and choose the correct word to go in the blank.

**Example:**

Sarah lost her book. "Did you see _____ book?" her friend Tim asked their teacher.

**A** Sarahs

**B** Sarahes

**C** Sarah

**D** Sarah's

**Answer:**

**D** Sarah's

**108** We saw one deer in the field, and three more ____ in the woods

**A** deers

**B** deere

**C** deer

**D** deerses

**109** This is my _____ bracelet.

**A** aunts

**B** aunt

**C** aunt's

**D** auntses

**110** We watched the _____ land on our pond.

**A** geese

**B** gooses

**C** goose

**D** geeses

**111** That is my English _____ book.

**A** teachers

**B** teachers'

**C** teacher's

**D** teacherses

**Directions:** Read each sentence and choose the letter underneath a verb.

**Example:**

He ate cake today.
**A**  **B**  **C**  **D**

**A** He

**B** ate

**C** cake

**D** today

**Answer:**

**B** ate

**112** <u>Jill</u> <u>hoped</u> that she would get a
    **A**   **B**

<u>horse</u> for her <u>birthday</u>.
  **C**         **D**

**A** Jill

**B** hoped

**C** horse

**D** birthday

**113** <u>Harry</u> <u>raced</u> up the hill <u>toward</u> his
     **A**    **B**          **C**

<u>school</u> yard.
  **D**

**A** Harry

**B** raced

**C** toward

**D** school

**114** <u>Yes,</u> <u>I</u> <u>know</u> what <u>time</u> it is.
    **A** **B** **C**      **D**

**A** Yes

**B** I

**C** know

**D** time

**115** <u>The</u> <u>wild</u> <u>horse</u> <u>is</u> mine.
    **A**   **B**   **C**   **D**

**A** The

**B** wild

**C** horse

**D** is

**Directions:** Read the sentences below and choose the correct pronoun to go in the blank.

**Example:**

George looked under his bed, but _____ could not find his puppy.

**A** he

**B** his

**C** him

**D** it

**Answer:**

**A** he

**116** If he doesn't do _____ homework, he will need to work harder tomorrow.

**A** he

**B** his

**C** her

**D** its

**117** Susie is in a hurry to make _____ bed.

    **A** she

    **B** he

    **C** hers

    **D** her

**Directions:** Read the sentence. Then choose the correct pronoun to fit in the blank.

**Example:**

    Jim likes to eat pizza. _____ likes pizza.

    **A** She

    **B** He

    **C** Her

    **D** Him

**Answer:**

    **B** He

**118** Cassie is an excellent tennis player. _____ plays tennis very well.

    **A** She

    **B** Her

    **C** He

    **D** Him

**119** Paige and Betsy love to work on science projects. _____ love science.

    **A** Hers      **B** They

    **C** Their      **D** She

**120** Joe and Ben are going to play basketball. They will play with _____ ball.

    **A** them      **B** him

    **C** yours      **D** their

**Directions:** Choose the sentence that is written correctly.

**Example:**

    **A** My dog Sammie is pretty, but that dog is prettier, and Karen's dog is prettiest of all.

    **B** It's cold than it was yesterday, but not as colder as it will be tomorrow.

    **C** This game is hard than I thought it would be.

    **D** This candy is good, but that one is gooder.

**Answer:**

    **A** My dog Sammie is pretty, but that dog is prettier, and Karen's dog is prettiest of all.

**121**  **A**  My dog is tired today, but yesterday he was even tireder.

     **B**  Jared says that division is hard, but Sam thinks decimals are harder.

     **C**  This is a pretty hat, but that hat is even prettiest.

     **D**  Yesterday it is hot, but two weeks ago it is even hotter.

**122**  **A**  Chili tastes good, but that soup is more better.

     **B**  I think my dog is the bestest pet in the class.

     **C**  John's cat is not as smart as Sally's.

     **D**  Justin is going to sang a pretty song.

**Directions:** Read each pair of sentences. Choose the sentence that best combines the two sentences into one.

**Example:**

Owls come out only at night. They hunt for insects and small rodents.

     **A**  Owls come out only at night to hunt for insects and small rodents.

     **B**  Owls come out only at night or hunt for insects and small rodents.

     **C**  Owls come out only at night but don't hunt for insects and small rodents.

     **D**  Owls come out only at night, hunt for insects, and small rodents.

**Answer:**

     **A**  Owls come out only at night to hunt for insects and small rodents.

**123**  Pumpkins make Halloween fun. So do scary ghosts.

     **A**  Pumpkins and scary ghosts make Halloween fun.

     **B**  Pumpkins but not ghosts make Halloween fun.

     **C**  Pumpkins, ghosts, make Halloween fun.

     **D**  Pumpkins or ghosts make Halloween fun.

**124**  Badgers are great diggers. They spend lots of time digging.

     **A**  Badgers like to dig and dig lots of time.

     **B**  Badgers are great diggers who spend lots of time digging.

     **C**  Badgers like to dig they spend lots of time doing that.

     **D**  Baders are diggers who like to dig.

Cut along dashed line.

GO

**125** Wolves talk to other wolves by howling. Their howls let others know where their territory is.

   **A** Wolves howl to other wolves to talk.

   **B** Wolves howl to talk and let other wolves know where their territory is.

   **C** Wolves have territory and they howl.

   **D** Wolves howl and have territory.

Cut along dashed line.

STOP

# READING COMPREHENSION

**Directions:** Read the following stories and then answer the questions that follow the stories.

## Coyotes

Coyotes are very smart animals. Many ranchers don't like coyotes because they think the animals kill lambs and calves. But coyotes always manage to avoid the ranchers' traps. If a coyote sees a person, it just trots away. Their fur blends in with the ground and bushes.

**Example:**

Coyotes are very _____.

**A** sneaky

**B** smart

**C** dull

**D** lazy

**Answer:**

**B** smart

126 What is this passage mostly about?

  **A** What coyotes eat

  **B** the problems ranchers have

  **C** where coyotes live

  **D** how smart coyotes are

127 How do coyotes avoid humans?

  **A** They run fast.

  **B** Their fur blends in with their surroundings.

  **C** They hide in holes.

  **D** They don't live near people.

128 What happens when ranchers set traps for coyotes?

  **A** The coyotes get caught.

  **B** The coyotes avoid the traps.

  **C** The coyotes see the traps.

  **D** The coyotes hear the traps.

129 What would another good title for this passage be?

  **A** Coyotes: Very Smart Animals

  **B** Where Do Coyotes Live?

  **C** Ranchers: A Hard Life

  **D** What Is a Coyote?

## PURR-FECT

Some experts think that cats purr when they are happy, such as when you are petting them and they curl up in your lap.

Their throat muscles relax, and their vocal cords loosen. As they breathe, the vocal cords vibrate; this makes a purring sound. However, some people say that cats also purr when they are afraid or in pain. Some people think the purr is not coming from the throat. Only cats really know why they purr.

**130** What is the main idea of the passage?

   **A** What a cat's purr means

   **B** how to play with cats

   **C** how many lives a cat has

   **D** cats in myth and magic

**131** How do some scientists think a cat purrs?

   **A** Their stomach makes a noise when they are happy.

   **B** When they are relaxed, their muscles loosen and their vocal cords vibrate.

   **C** The cat's tongue vibrates when it's happy.

   **D** The cat's stomach rumbles when it is hungry.

**132** The passage says: "the vocal cords <u>vibrate</u>." What does <u>vibrate</u> mean in this sentence?

   **A** move very quickly back and forth

   **B** make a sound

   **C** tremble

   **D** scream

### Getting Ready for School

It was time for Jim to get ready for school. First, he got out of bed. Then he got out his clothes and placed them on the bed. He ran into the bathroom and found his toothbrush and washcloth. As he scrubbed his face, he grinned. "Dad is going to be really surprised!" Jim told himself. His dad had been upset lately that he had been dawdling in the morning. His mother had often had to call him three or four times before he responded and got out of bed. He was often late for school. But this morning he got himself up and ready for school. He was trying to show his parents that he was responsible.

**Example:**

   Why did Jim find his toothbrush?

   **A** He wanted to take a bath.

   **B** He needed to brush his teeth.

   **C** He needed to wash his face.

   **D** He liked to play in the water.

**Answer:**

   **B** He needed to brush his teeth.

**133** What did Jim do first in the story?

   **A** lined up his clothes

   **B** found his toothbrush

   **C** got out of bed

   **D** washed his face

Cut along dashed line.

**134** Why did Jim want to get up by himself?

   **A** He liked to play in the morning.

   **B** He wanted to have lots of time to wash.

   **C** He wanted to make his bed.

   **D** He wanted to show his parents he could be responsible.

---

**135** The story uses the word <u>responsible</u>. What does the word <u>responsible</u> mean in this passage?

   **A** good with animals

   **B** smart and funny

   **C** capable and mature

   **D** popular

---

### The Last Day

Emma walked slowly into the school building. Today was her last day at her old school, where she had gone all her life. All of her friends were at this school. In the new school, she wouldn't know anyone. She'd be The New Kid. How she would miss this old building! Tears pricked her eyes as she walked toward her old classroom for the last time. Would any of her friends even miss her? No one had even bothered to walk her to school today. Would they realize they may never see her again? As she walked into her class, she heard an enormous cheer. "Surprise!" her friends cried.

Emma stared. The room was decorated with streamers and balloons. "Good-bye and good luck" signs were hanging from the window. All her friends were standing together smiling and waving. Emma laughed out loud.

**Example:**

   Why is Emma sad?

   **A** She's worried about a test.

   **B** She is new at school.

   **C** She's going to miss her old friends.

   **D** She forgot her books.

**Answer:**

   **C** She's going to miss her old friends.

---

**136** How does Emma feel?

   **A** excited about being in a new school

   **B** sad about leaving the old school

   **C** tired from carrying her books

   **D** happy about being The New Kid

---

**137** Where does this story take place?

   **A** in the auditorium

   **B** in a classroom

   **C** in the cafeteria

   **D** in the gym

GO

**138** What is the classroom like?

A silent and empty

B noisy and crowded

C dark and scary

D bright and hot

**139** How does Emma probably feel when she sees the classroom?

A angry

B happy

C lonesome

D mad

## Story

Penguins have bodies built for the coldest weather on earth. Their oily feathers lie close together, which keeps out the cold wind and keeps their body heat in. They have a thick layer of fat all over their bodies. In cold water they are still comfortable.

**140** What is the best title for this passage?

A How Penguins Live in the Cold

B Antarctic Animals

C I Like Penguins

D Winter's Cold

**Directions:** Read the question and choose the correct answer.

**141** What is a book titled *The Mystery of the Haunted Stable* most likely about?

A a myth about gods and goddesses

B a mystery involving horses

C a collection of frightening tales

D a sad story about a family who loses everything in a fire

**Directions:** Read the following passage, and choose the sentence describing what would logically happen next.

Sally straightened her back and picked up the saw. Carefully, she placed the board on the sawhorse and began to saw. Her father waved to her from his position at the top of the playhouse. It wouldn't be long now before the roof was on! Sally laughed as the board fell apart at her feet.

**142** A She sat down and ate some lunch.

B She picked up the boards and took them over to her father who was waiting to nail them into place.

C She picked up a paintbrush and started to paint the windowsill.

D She unsaddled the pony and walked away.

Cut along dashed line.

GO

**Directions:** Read the following passage. Choose the statement that best describes what the story will probably be about.

The wind howled through the forest, and the night creatures scurried home. The trees crashed against the old house, and a shutter creaked mournfully on its squeaky hinges.

143 **A** The story will probably be a scary mystery.

**B** The story will probably be very funny.

**C** The story will probably be about happy farm animals.

**D** The story will probably be about science facts.

Young Prince George sat down at the exam table with a sigh. He just had to score well on this test. From the day he was born, he had been groomed to take over the throne. Still, he knew his father was expecting him to do well in school first.

144 **A** This story will probably be a biography about the prince.

**B** This story will probably be a factual article about education.

**C** This story will probably make people laugh.

**D** This story will probably be about a happy peasant family.

**Directions:** Read this passage and then answer the question.

Paul was having a hard time at school. He did not read very well because he had some problems recognizing some of the letters. He was very bright, but reading was hard for him. The other kids teased him for being slow.

**Example:**

Why did the kids tease Paul?

**A** because he was mean

**B** because he seemed slow

**C** because he was spoiled

**D** because he was poor

**Answer:**

**A** because he seemed slow

145 Why did Paul have trouble in class?

**A** He was dumb.

**B** He was bad.

**C** He had some problems with reading.

**D** He spoke French.

Cut along dashed line.

STOP

# LITERARY GENRES

**Directions:** Read the following sentences. Three of the sentences are opinions. Choose the sentence that is a fact.

**146** **A** Ferris wheels are fun to ride.

**B** Ferris wheels have seats.

**C** It's scary at the top of a Ferris wheel.

**D** When the wind blows, Ferris wheels are the scariest ride in the park.

**147** **A** John Brown is running for president.

**B** John Brown is a bad man.

**C** John Brown is not very good in politics.

**D** No one trusts John Brown.

**Directions:** Choose the correct answers for the following questions.

**148** Which of these sentences is true?

**A** Horses can do tricks.

**B** Humans have walked on Mars.

**C** Cats can speak.

**D** Unicorns exist.

**149** Which of these sentences is based on fantasy?

**A** Humans have two hands.

**B** Giants can climb down bean stalks.

**C** Human beings can sing long songs.

**D** Jets fly in the air.

**Directions:** Read the following passage. Choose the correct answer to each question.

George Washington was born on February 22. He was the very first President of the United States. He was also the leader of the American Army in the war for independence. He has been called the "father of our country."

**150** George Washington was

**A** the first politician in space.

**B** the first President of the United States.

**C** the inventor of electricity.

**D** the first king of the United States.

GO →

155

**151** Washington was called

    **A** the "father of our country."

    **B** the "leader" of the British.

    **C** a "terrific" father.

    **D** "father of the year."

**Directions:** Read each poem. Answer the questions that follow each poem.

### The Land of Counterpane
By Robert Louis Stevenson

When I was sick and lay a-bed,
I had two pillows at my head,
And all my toys beside me lay,
To keep me happy all the day.

And sometimes for an hour or so
I watched my leaden soldiers go,
With different uniforms and drills,
Among the bed-clothes, through the hills;

And sometimes sent my ships in fleets
All up and down among the sheets;
Or brought my trees and houses out,
And planted cities all about.

I was the giant great and still
That sits upon the pillow-hill,
And sees before him, dale and plain,
The pleasant land of counterpane.

**152** What does the author mean by the words "leaden soldiers"?

    **A** The soldiers were tired.

    **B** The soldiers were made of lead.

    **C** The soldiers were plastic.

    **D** The soldiers were toys.

**153** From this poem, you can tell

    **A** that the poet had a great imagination.

    **B** that the poet was sick a lot.

    **C** that the poet doesn't like to sleep.

    **D** that it's Christmas time.

### Twinkle, Twinkle Little Star
By Jane Taylor

Twinkle, twinkle, little star,
How I wonder what you are.
Up above the world so high,
Like a diamond in the sky.

When the blazing sun is gone,
When he nothing shines upon,
Then you show your little light,
Twinkle, twinkle, all the night.

Then the trav'ller in the dark,
Thanks you for your tiny spark,
He could not see which way to go,
If you did not twinkle so.

In the dark blue sky you keep,
And often thro' my curtains peep,
For you never shut your eye,
Till the sun is in the sky.

'Tis your bright and tiny spark,
Lights the trav'ller in the dark:
Tho' I know not what you are,
Twinkle, twinkle, little star.

**154** What does the author compare a star to?

    **A** a diamond

    **B** the sun

    **C** the moon

    **D** the sky

Cut along dashed line.

**155** Why does the traveler thank the stars?

    **A** because they light his way

    **B** because he likes to look at them

    **C** because he's afraid of the dark

    **D** because he is polite

# STUDY SKILLS

**Directions:** For the list of words in each question, choose the word that would come next in correct alphabetical order from the choices below.

**Example:**

country   dirt   friend

**A** always

**B** been

**C** cane

**D** guess

**Answer:**

**D** guess

---

**156** anyone   excited   school

**A** bat

**B** when

**C** rat

**D** meaning

---

**157** been   before   beginning

**A** beat

**B** bar

**C** believer

**D** be

---

**158** wear   Wednesday   were

**A** western

**B** was

**C** weaver

**D** welt

---

**Directions :** Which word would you find on the following dictionary page, between the guide words *often* and *out*?

| often | out |
| --- | --- |
| | |

**Example:**

**A** off

**B** of

**C** ogle

**D** igloo

**Answer:**

**C** ogle

**159** **A** bout

**B** oink

**C** oval

**D** oxen

---

**Directions:** Choose the correct answer for the following questions.

**Example:**

Where would you look to find detailed information on the life and times of Albert Einstein?

**A** encyclopedia    **B** dictionary

**C** poetry book    **D** atlas

**Answer:**

**A** encyclopedia

---

**160** If Rachel wanted to find out the definition of <u>heaves</u> in her book on show horses, where would she look?

**A** index

**B** table of contents

**C** title page

**D** glossary

---

**161** If you were reading a book about germs and you wanted to find the page that contains a specific detail about germs, where would you look to find that page number?

**A** in the table of contents

**B** in the glossary

**C** in the index

**D** in the title page

---

**162** George wants to get a general idea of the topics covered in his book on trains. He would look in

**A** the table of contents.

**B** the glossary.

**C** the index.

**D** the title page.

STOP

# Answer Key for Sample Practice Test

**Vocabulary**

| | |
|---|---|
| 1 | D |
| 2 | A |
| 3 | B |
| 4 | D |
| 5 | D |
| 6 | C |

**Word Meanings in Context**

| | |
|---|---|
| 7 | B |
| 8 | C |
| 9 | B |
| 10 | B |
| 11 | D |
| 12 | C |
| 13 | C |
| 14 | C |
| 15 | C |

**Antonyms, Synonyms, and Homophones**

| | |
|---|---|
| 16 | B |
| 17 | C |
| 18 | A |
| 19 | C |
| 20 | D |
| 21 | C |
| 22 | A |
| 23 | D |
| 24 | A |

| | |
|---|---|
| 25 | D |
| 26 | D |
| 27 | A |
| 28 | C |
| 29 | C |
| 30 | A |
| 31 | B |
| 32 | D |
| 33 | C |
| 34 | D |
| 35 | C |
| 36 | C |
| 37 | A |
| 38 | B |
| 39 | D |
| 40 | B |
| 41 | D |
| 42 | D |
| 43 | B |
| 44 | C |
| 45 | C |
| 46 | C |
| 47 | B |
| 48 | B |
| 49 | B |
| 50 | D |
| 51 | A |

**Word Sounds**

| | |
|---|---|
| 52 | A |
| 53 | A |
| 54 | C |

| | |
|---|---|
| 55 | B |
| 56 | A |
| 57 | B |
| 58 | C |
| 59 | A |
| 60 | D |
| 61 | D |
| 62 | D |
| 63 | A |
| 64 | D |
| 65 | C |
| 66 | D |
| 67 | A |
| 68 | B |
| 69 | B |
| 70 | C |
| 71 | D |

**Spelling**

| | |
|---|---|
| 72 | B |
| 73 | D |
| 74 | B |
| 75 | C |
| 76 | A |
| 77 | D |
| 78 | A |
| 79 | D |
| 80 | C |
| 81 | A |
| 82 | B |
| 83 | C |
| 84 | A |

| | |
|---|---|
| 85 | B |
| 86 | A |
| 87 | C |
| 88 | B |
| 89 | C |
| 90 | D |
| 91 | B |
| 92 | A |
| 93 | C |
| 94 | D |
| 95 | C |

**Capitalization and Punctuation**

| | |
|---|---|
| 96 | A |
| 97 | D |
| 98 | C |
| 99 | A |
| 100 | B |
| 101 | D |
| 102 | B |
| 103 | D |
| 104 | C |
| 105 | D |
| 106 | C |
| 107 | B |

**Grammar Rules**

| | |
|---|---|
| 108 | C |
| 109 | C |
| 110 | A |
| 111 | C |

| | | | | | | | |
|---|---|---|---|---|---|---|---|
| 112 | B | | | 139 | B | 152 | B |
| 113 | B | **Reading** | | 140 | A | 153 | A |
| 114 | C | **Comprehension** | | 141 | B | 154 | A |
| 115 | D | 126 | D | 142 | B | 155 | A |
| 116 | B | 127 | B | 143 | A | | |
| 117 | D | 128 | B | 144 | A | **Study Skills** | |
| 118 | A | 129 | A | 145 | C | 156 | B |
| 119 | B | 130 | A | | | 157 | C |
| 120 | D | 131 | B | **Literary Genres** | | 158 | A |
| 121 | B | 132 | A | 146 | B | 159 | B |
| 122 | C | 133 | C | 147 | A | 160 | D |
| 123 | A | 134 | D | 148 | A | 161 | C |
| 124 | B | 135 | C | 149 | B | 162 | A |
| 125 | B | 136 | B | 150 | B | | |
| | | 137 | B | 151 | A | | |
| | | 138 | B | | | | |

# WORKSHEET